HANDBOOK FOR DOCTOR OF MINISTRY PROJECTS

An Approach to
Structured Observation
of Ministry

Richard E. Davies, Ph.D.

UNIVERSITY
PRESS OF
AMERICA

LANHAM • NEW YORK • LONDON

Copyright © 1984 by

University Press of America,® Inc.
4501 Forbes Boulevard, Suite 200
Lanham, Maryland 20706

3 Henrietta Street
London WC2E 8LU England

Library of Congress Cataloging in Publication Data

Davies, Richard E., 1941-
Handbook for doctor of ministry projects.

Bibliography: p.
1. Doctor of ministry degree. 2. Dissertations,
Academic. I. Title.
BV165.D38 1984   207'.2   83-23593
ISBN 0-8191-3763-4 (alk. paper)
ISBN 0-8191-3764-2 (pbk. : alk. paper)

ACKNOWLEDGEMENTS

Grateful acknowledgement is made for permission to quote from the following:

A Bible Skills Workshop, Clyde D. Flannery. Unpublished doctoral dissertation (D. Min.), Christian Theological Seminary, 1976. Used with permission of the author.

A Project in Leadership Development for a Local Church's Ministry of Evangelism Through Small Group Interaction, William L. Bass. Unpublished doctoral dissertation (D. Min.), Christian Theological Seminary, 1977. Used with permission of the author.

"A Perspective for New Researchers in Religious Education." William A. Koppe. An unpublished paper. 1982. Used with permission of the author.

A Study of Factors in the Understanding of Salvation-Related Concepts. Jerry A. Privette. Ed.D. dissertation, Southern Baptist Theological Seminary, 1972. Used with permission of the author.

Catholicism, Richard P. McBrien. Copyright © 1980 by Richard P. McBrien. Published by Winston Press, Inc. All rights reserved. Used with permission of the publisher.

Communicating God's Character to Children. William Boyd Fortney. Unpublished Master's Thesis, Dallas Theological Seminary, 1973. Used with permission of the author.

Dissertation Abstracts International, published with permission of University Microfilms International, 300 North Zeeb Road, Ann Arbor, Michigan 48106.

Essentials of Evangelical Theology, Volume Two: Life, Ministry, and Hope. Donald G. Bloesch. Harper and Row Publishers, San Francisco, CA. Copyright © 1979. Used with permission of the publisher.

Evaluation Research: Methods of Assessing Program Effectiveness, Carol H. Weiss. Copyright © 1972 Adapted by permission of Prentice-Hall, Inc., publisher.

TABLE OF CONTENTS

The Purpose of this Book
The Scope of this Book
The Value of Empirical Research
What the Researcher Does

Program Evaluation
    Routine Ministerial Program Evaluation
    Evaluation Tools
    Goals
    An Example of Program Evaluation
    Evaluation Design
Treatment Effects
    Control Groups
    Time Series
    An Example of Treatment Effects Research
    A Suggestion
Survey Research
    Survey Sampling
    How to Select a Random Sample
    Other Questions
    Data Analysis
    Example of Correlation in Survey Research
Case Studies
    Example of a Model: Communication
    Example of a Model: Innovation
    Example of a Model: Ministry
    Objective Observation
    Consider Alternatives
One More Example of Program Evaluation:
Analyzing Some Worship Preferences

Writing Questions
Likert Response: An Approach to Opinion
Scaling: Two Questions are Better Than One
Making a Scale: Sermon Response
Question Formats
Maximizing Survey Response

Where to Find Tests
Standardized Tests
Some Potentially Useful Tests
    Purpose in Life
    Moral Development
    Ministerial Job Satisfaction
    "A Study of Values"
Semantic Differential
Group Tests
Content Analysis
Interaction Analysis

How To Approach Statistics
Statistical Concepts and Definitions
One Basic Distinction: Two Kinds of Analysis
Another Basic Distinction: Levels of Measurement
How to Read and Use a Basic Formula:
    Standard Deviation
Standard Deviation and Normal Distribution
Correlation
    Pearson Product-Moment Correlation Coefficient
    Ordinal Data Correlation
    More Than Two Columns of Ordinal Data
    The Meaning of Correlation
When are Two Numbers Different?
Student's t Test: A Test of Differences
Chi-Square: An Inferential Tool

Reporting Percentages
Notes on Surveying Priorities
Other Techniques for Studying Phenomena

PREFACE

Take the title of this book seriously, particularly the word "handbook." As the author, I hope the book reads well, but I recognize that some chapters are not good narrative with beginning, middle and end allowing for an easy summary. Instead, some chapters are collections of ideas and references. Thus, the word "handbook." Not all of the ideas will serve you well, but I hope some of them will.

The subtitle refers to "structured observation." These words describe what I think you are to do in developing a D.Min. project. You are to observe something (and draw conclusions). The phenomena you observe will be in the "real world," as opposed to a literary or historical world. In seminary, you probably learned how to observe historical worlds. Furthermore, as a D. Min. student, you probably are quite good at preaching and counseling, skills that require actue observation of daily life. But "structured observation" is different.

With the term "structured observation," I intend to convey the necessity of observing phenomena in such a way that anyone using the same tools of observation, under the same conditions, will probably see the same thing. The common word is "objectivity," but the word is so "loaded," it seemed best not to use it in a title. Besides, the descriptive term "structured observation" might help you focus on a process, rather than some abstract outcome.

A reader of the manuscript was quite critical of the "research" orientation of this book, saying "its major flaw . . . is its confusion of an act of ministry with an act of research." I see this complaint as being so serious as to require comment. If I understand the comment, it refers to a distinction which I intentionally did not discuss in the first version, feeling it was of theoretical, but not of practical significance.

Someone (I don't know who) has suggested that behavioral/social research should be seen in two categories: "conclusion-oriented" and "decision-

xi

oriented." Please don't blame me for the very opague jargon. Here's what the terms mean: A conclusion-oriented research project will seek to verify or extend a theory. In other words, it will try to reach a universal conclusion. The best Ph.D. dissertations are examples of conclusion-oriented research. A decision-oriented research project will seek evidence to decide which of several options a person should follow. Such research is focused on a fairly specific issue, and not particularly concerned with universals. The best examples are probably found in market research.

Of course, few research projects will fit neatly into one or the other category, but it seems to me that D. Min. projects, involving "structured observation of acts of ministry," will be "decision-oriented research." As research, it will involve the careful use of recognized tools of observation. An "act of ministry," by itself, is the sort of thing you do all the time. I presume your motivation for pursuing the D. Min. is to improve your ministerial skills. the way to get better is to analyze carefully what you do, using research tools. You can also benefit from analyzing the people with whom you work, the institution in which you work, or the community around you. And you may find your ministry benefiting most from a more abstract, "conclusion-oriented" project. The possibilities are limitless, and in this book, I have attempted to provide some inspiration and guidance for many of the possibilities.

By the way, if you are struggling with a topic, and find yourself needing a break, you might enjoy an "article" by LeRoy Koopman in LEADERSHIP, Spring 1982 (vol. 3, #2), pp. 62-63. The title: "Twenty Unresearched Seminary Thesis Topics."

Bibliographic Note

As I was getting this book ready for publication, I received word of a resource you might find useful:

Silverman, William. "Bibliography of Measurement Techniques Used in the Social Scientific Study of Religion," Psychological Documents, 1983, (Ms. #2539). 90 pp.

Although I have not seen it, I know that Silverman has been working on it for several years. According to the notice, it includes 292 references to "tests" (as they are called in this book) and 170 references to questionnaires. Silverman's bibliography can be ordered from: Psychological Documents, American Psychological Association, 1200 17th Street, N.W., Washington, DC 20036. A microfiche copy costs $3.50. A paper copy costs $14.50.

CHAPTER I

INTRODUCTION: D. MIN. RESEARCH AND THIS BOOK

The Purpose of this Book

This book is intended to give some assistance to people who are planning to write a thesis for the doctor of Ministry (D. Min.) degree. Others who are interested in an overview of the social/ behavioral approach to the study of religion might also find it useful, but D. Min. students form a distinct category of researchers whose special problems have not yet been addressed in print.

The need for a book such as the present one grows from the nature of the D. Min. The D. Min. degree is intended to be an advanced professional degree for clergy and certain other religious professionals. It is granted by schools of theology, and most schools require a graduate level professional degree (normally the Master of Divinity) along with a minimum amount of pastoral or related experience as prerequisite to being admitted to the D. Min. program. Since the D. Min. is to be practical, thesis research will generally involve observation of, and possible experimentation in, the parish or other pastoral situation. Such empirical research will be in addition to appropriate biblical/theological/ philosophical research.

Most clergy have no background in social/behavioral science research, while the background required for admission to the degree program means that they are probably quite competent to do biblical/theological/philosophical and his-torical research. Because professional experience is also normally required for admission to the degree program, D. Min. students also have a practical understanding of issues in ministry. This book attempts to address them as professionals who understand professional issues, and help them see how such issues might be dealt with by applying social/behavioral science methods to situations as a complement to theological/philosophical and professional analyses of the situations.

1

The book includes many concrete examples intended to illustrate how social/behavioral science techniques might be used. The examples might also inspire ideas for new D. Min. thesis topics.

Much of this book is written in the first and second persons, singular, because it is written by me and intended for you, the reader.

The Scope of this Book

There is a built-in frustration in writing a book such as this. Much more should be said than can be said in a brief handbook. My hope is to have told you enough so you can find necessary additional information with little trouble. In some ways, this book is a bibliographic essay, and there are some books you will certainly want to refer to in addition to this one. Among them are Kerlinger (1973), Robinson and Shaver (1973), and the Mental Measurements Yearbooks by Buros (e.g., 1978). You will also want to refer to some introductory textbooks in statistical analysis.

As has been said, this book deals with empirical research. The assumption is that you are well trained in techniques for research in the humanities. Furthermore, there are adequate handbooks to guide you in theologically oriented research in the humanities. For example, if you decide that your research needs to be historical, look up the bibliography by Birkos and Tambs (1975). they have a chapter devoted to "research methods in history" that includes 158 books and articles published between 1965 and 1973. You may also want to look at Nearby History: Exploring the Past Around You by David E. Kyvig and Myron A. Marty. Order from American Association for State and Local History, 708 Berry Road, Nashville, Tennessee 37204. $15.95. It was recommended by Martin Marty in his Christian Century column (March 9, 1983, p. 231).

The present book has a definite emphasis on quantitative research, even though it is also useful to do qualitative empirical research studies. The reason for this is partly a reflection of "the state of the art." Most of the research techniques discussed here have been developed in the 20th century

2

(even though they have earlier philosophical antecedents), and in this century much more work has been done on procedures and standards for quantitative research than qualitative research. Another reason for emphasizing quantitative research is that quantitative techniques can be used as a background for qualitative techniques. A general understanding of quantitative research techniques is a form of literacy you will find useful in many contexts.

Recently some researchers have expressed a need for new approaches to qualitative empirical research. In light of this, there may be some significant new publications on qualitative research over the next few years. If you sense a need to do qualitative research for your D. Min. thesis, you should definitely read John K. Smith's (1983) article on the philosophical background of research, and the excellent bibliographic essay on qualitative research by Lemish and Lemish (1982). A recent textbook on qualitative research is Bogdan and Biklen (1982). It includes an 11 page bibliography.

This book is also intended to provide a guide through the process of selecting a topic, formulating a question, designing a study, and collecting, analyzing and interpreting data. Throughout the book, I have drawn examples from actual research. I hope these examples will not only illustrate particular points in the book, but will suggest directions for your research.

The book is too brief to deal with the final phase of your thesis, writing, but don't forget that writing is possibly the most important part of the project. When you first plan your degree program, you should budget more than adequate time to do the writing. Writing always takes longer than you think it will.

The Hawthorne Effect

Before you get deeply involved in planning your research, there is one serious problem you will inevitably confront. Perhaps it is good to mention it now, rather than later.

In 1939, Roethisberger and Dickson published the results of an extensive research study on management and the worker. One of the frustrating things they found was that every change seemed to increase group productivity. For example, adequate lighting increased productivity, but so did reduced lighting. They concluded that paying special attention to people leads them to change their behavior (Mosteller, 1968, p. 115). This may not sound surprising, but it has serious implications for D. Min. research.

Most likely, the members of your church want you to succeed in getting the D. Min. If you implement a special program, organize a special committee, or start a special class in your church as part of your D. Min. research, the people who are asked to participate will probably respond atypically. They will probably devote more effort than normal to their participation. You may conclude that your project was a total success and be disappointed later in your ministry when a repetition of the project doesn't work as well as it did during the research period.

Roethlisberger and Dickson did their research at the Western Electric Company's Hawthorne Plant, and since that time, this problem has been called the "Hawthorne effect." There is no formula for neutralizing the Hawthorne effect, but you certainly need to be aware of it. Enyart (1978, p. 90) encountered the Hawthorne effect in his D. Min. project, and this is how he reported it:

> The fact that I had visited each of these people in their job settings certainly had an influence on their feelings toward the sermons. In retrospect I wish I had included some persons in the group who had not participated with me in the interviews and the job visitations. It might have been interesting to see how the attitudes of these people differed from the ones I had visited on the job.

In the jargon of research, Enyart wished he had used a "control group." Indeed, he should have, but even control groups will not necessarily solve the problem of the Hawthorne Effect.

4

The Value of Empirical Research

Empirical research depends on conceptualizing and theorizing. We can only study those phenomena that we have thought deeply about. The exceptions to this principle are rare.

Once we understand what we want to study, empirical techniques may provide us with information that challenges our preconceptions. If this happens, and if we have followed proper research techniques, we should rejoice over having learned something new, even if it causes us to revise the way we think about the phenomenon we are studying.

All too often, empirical research that violates preconceptions is ignored, sometimes with harmful effects. The case of the Susan B. Anthony dollar is a notorious example. Professional surveys done before and after the coin was designed indicated that the public would not accept it (Armbrister, 1980). Those in charge of the project chose to ignore the surveys and produced the ill-fated coin at great expense to the U.S. public. You can probably think of analogous examples within the life of your denomination.

We are, no doubt, called to dream dreams and see visions. But visions and dreams should be subject to tests of reality.

In October, 1982, William Koppe, a researcher on the National Staff of the Lutheran Church in America, presented a brief paper on the nature of research in the religious community to participants in the annual meeting of the Association of Professors and Researchers in Religious Education. He said some important things and said them well:

A PERSPECTIVE FOR NEW RESEARCHERS IN RELIGIOUS EDUCATION

William A. Koppe

A friend of mine discovered that a high percentage of the members in LCA congregations approved of increasing the numbers of minorities among our members and as congregational leaders and that

5

they generally approved of an increase of women as leaders. Well, it ain't necessarily so!

Because of the psychological quirks of people who answer questionnaires, I knew that these findings are not so simple. First, people respond, in part, in terms of ways they are expected to respond. That's called <u>social desirability.</u> Secondly, some people are optimistic raters, and some are doubtful raters. The compensation for this is an "<u>ipsative correction.</u>"

Corrected for these two biases, the truth seems to be that people do indeed approve of such changes in their congregations <u>up until they believe they are really going to happen!</u> Then they have their doubts.

The fact of the matter is that all of our data, expressed as percentages, factors, F tests, correlations, or whatever cannot ever be called truth. These findings are only clues to truth. It is only when we gather together these clues from a variety of sources and situations that we can construct a "picture" of truth which is, in fact, a best guess based on the clues available. Some call these best guesses, <u>Theories</u>. Therein lies the dilemma of all researchers.

Our job is to find truth--relevant truth-- but, if we are honest with ourselves--and we experienced researchers have not always been honest--we must admit that we are working on the basis of "best guesses" which are forever subject to change without notice. The quest for truth <u>is</u> our central task. It is our obligation to recogni<u>ze</u> that all truth is theory--a best guess about reality!

But the truth we find is useless unless it is communicated to others. It must be understood. From my research on "How Persons Grow in Christian Community," I became convinced that children learned what they expected to learn! In fact, how persons relate to their congregations is profoundly affected by their expectancies of the church. I was shocked to discover that a great many persons couldn't make any sense out of that truth. It doesn't tell anything about moral development, teacher training, or curriculum development.

If the truth we find is to be understood, we must
"play the role of the other" so that we communicate
our understandings from the point of view of our
audience. Therein lies a risk. Once people really
understand what we are talking about--they may feel
threatened! "You mean I've been wrong all these
years?"

The fact of the matter is that we almost never
communicate "the truth, the whole truth, and nothing
but the truth." Given our audience we need to judge
which understanding of our truth needs to be
communicated. Where does this truth fit into the lives
and decisions of those we are addressing?

I think of research as a T-U-B. It must be
true, T. It must be understood, U. And it also must
be believable, B. Make any generalization you care to
make and someone in the crowd will describe an
exception to the case. There goes your credibility!

I believe we researchers in religious education
are involved in a serious business. Sometimes we get
so deeply involved in our computerized SPSS, our
sampling techniques, and our carefully worded
questionnaires that we fail to involve others in our
quest for truth and in our belief that this truth will
improve education. I believe that one reason our
research may not be believable is that we fail to
report our findings in the context of the overall
problem.

We need to learn the popularized form of
reporting exemplified by the Scientific American or
the National Geographic. Although we cannot expect
people to be patient enough to sit still for a
presentation of the history of the problem, we can, in
a sense, set the stage so that our readers or
listeners are ready for what is to come. It is the
art of the short-story writer.

We, the older members of the profession have
often found ourselves, first, on quests for truth no
one else cares about, second, communicating only to
those who already understand and third, expecting
people to believe just because we say so.

I would hope that you new researchers will first,
struggle with the Truth that matters to professors,

7

curriculum developers, and church school teachers, second, help them to Understand that portion of the truth that is relevant to their work and third, be sensitive to the context in which they are working so that the report of your research will be supportive and consequently, Believable.

October 4, 1982.

CHAPTER II

WHAT KIND OF RESEARCH SHALL I DO?
SOME USEFUL APPROACHES

There is a necessary connection between deciding what approach to use in research and deciding what you want to find out, but for the sake of simplicity, this chapter will deal with research approaches, and the next chapter will be devoted to identifying a topic for study. Research design is a large topic, but the approaches introduced in this chapter will be relevant to most D. Min. research.

Program Evaluation

The purpose of evaluation research is to measure the effects of a program against the goals it set out to accomplish as a means of contributing to subsequent decision making about the program and improving future programming. (Weiss, 1972, p. 4)

A majority of D. Min. projects will involve program evaluation, because most projects in ministry involve doing something in the life of the congregation, the community, or in the pattern of ministerial work. These are "programs," and for a thesis, it is not sufficient to simply plan and execute the program, no matter how sophisticated it may be or how much work was involved in the planning and implementation. A thesis should include a relatively objective assessment of how well the program functioned, at what points it might be improved, and how the improvement might be implemented.

Good program evaluation is expensive in terms of time and effort. Evaluation in D. Min. projects will probably not be financially expensive, although you should set aside some money for the possible expense of printing questionnaires, mailing, extra secretarial help, and possibly the purchase and scoring of standardized tests or travel expenses for

9

denominational staff members or other consultants. Even though the dollar outlay need not be great, the total expense should not be underestimated. Budget adequate time for evaluation planning, and put whatever limitations you need to on your program so that formal evaluation can be built in.

Routine Ministerial Program Evaluation

It is possible that ministers are more time conscious than almost any other group of people. This is because there are so many demands made on them that they must continually assess what is and what is not worth doing, and how much time particular activities are worth. In other words, ministers routinely do some sort of program evaluation.

Most ministerial program evaluation is subjective. In addition to the minister's feeling about how well the program functioned, there is a subjective evaluation of how smoothly the program was implemented. Who cooperated? Who said they would cooperate, but didn't? Who declined to cooperate, but finally did? Who gave no support at all? This sort of evaluation is important, and has some validity. Furthermore, most programs do not merit more than subjective evaluation. But although subjective comments should be included in the thesis, they should not be the backbone of thesis evaluation.

Ministerial program evaluation is also likely to come from the romantic tradition, so that if we can see that the program benefited one person, and didn't harm anyone, we pronounce the program to have been worthwhile. A strong philosophical/ theological case can be made for a stated goal of helping one person. The church does not define the "cost/benefit" ratio the way the business world does. But too often references to the one lost sheep or the single sparrow (Matt. 18:12, 10:29) are an ex post facto attempt to justify the energy devoted to a program that was really a failure. If your goal is to help one person, say so at the beginning and plan your evaluation accordingly.

Routine ministerial program evaluation is also based on selective responses. It is "human nature" that those who liked the program will say so, and those who did not will be silent (except for the person who is vocally against everything. "Every" congregation has one such person.)

In formal program evaluation, you hope to get equivalent responses from everyone involved, or from a representative sample of those involved.

Evaluation Tools

In some cases, the evaluation tools you use will grow out of your goals. For example, if you are doing a teaching project, some sort of test or tests will be among your evaluation tools. If your project involves small groups, you may turn to sociometry or interaction analysis for evaluation assistance. (See chapter 8 for an example of interaction analysis.)

There are also many evaluation tools that are independent of goals. Among these are participant evaluation questionnaires, independent expert observers, degree of participation (including attendance), and standardized tests.

Goals

You cannot evaluate if you do not have goals. Frequently, in church programs, our unstated goal is that "everyone should feel good about what happened," and frequently this is an appropriate goal. However, the goals of a D. Min. project should be more specific. If the goal is for "everyone to feel good," then everyone sets his or her own goal. In a project in ministry, you should take responsibility for the goals, and not simply leave them to the program participants. After all, it is _your_ project.

It would be appropriate to include a goal such as "every participant should feel that his or her needs were met," but this goes beyond the common unstated "feel good" goal. When you ask people if their perceived needs were met, you also find out what the specific perceived needs were, and if the needs should have been addressed by the project, then the project

11

can be modified on the basis of the evaluation response.

It is not always easy to specify goals. Cain and Hollister (1972, pp. 112 & 114) recognize this:

In the methodology of program evaluation which has been constructed, one of the principle tenets is that the first step in the analysis must be to specify the objectives of the program. Unfortunately, agreement on this principle has not facilitated its implementation, the problem being that few programs have a clearly defined single objective or even one dominant objective.

. . . it must be recognized that there are some important social action programs for which it is necessary to observe what a program is doing and, in the process of observation, identify what the objectives are.

This leads them to describe an iterative procedure that they call "search evaluation." In "search evaluation," the goals are defined as the project proceeds. It is their contention that "search evaluation" is the best sort of evaluation possible in some situations. If your project involves a large program that is difficult to define, you should study their article.

An Example of Program Evaluation

Selman and Lieberman (1975) published an evaluation study that is similar to what one might find in a good D. Min. project. They had developed some moral education materials for children in the early primary grades, and wanted to know how effective they were. They used groups of second grade pupils from different schools, middle and working class, and strictly middle class. There were three groups in each school, one taught by an expert, one taught by a lay person, and one used as a "control" for comparison.

The researchers developed an interview/test to gauge the moral maturity of second graders, and gave it to the students three times: (a) in the fall, before the instructional program, (b) in the winter, immediately after the program, and (c) at the end of the school year, to determine long term effects.

The program was effective, and showed long term effectiveness. It was at least as effective when taught by informed lay people as when taught by experts, and it was equally effective in both schools.

In spite of what seems to be resounding success, the authors display professional caution in noting the limits of their evaluation (p. 716):

> . . . it is obvious that in our experimental design it is impossible to sort out "teacher effects" from "intervention techniques." . . . for this reason alone, this can only be regarded as a pilot study. . . . another major limitation of this study is the use of only one evaluation procedure. . . given the amount of change in usage of the concept of moral intentions which occurred over the October-May period, it seems worthwhile to design and carry through research with a larger sample. . . .

Such professional caution and candor is likewise appropriate for D. Min. thesis work. If your project is at all similar in structure to this research by Selman and Lieberman, their article is worth study.

Evaluation Design

Isaac and Michael (1981, pp. 42-43) identified nine basic methods of research. They are "historical," "descriptive," "developmental" (study of growth or change over time), "case and field" (see section on case studies later in this chapter), "correlational" (study of how one thing relates to another, see section on correlation in chapter 9), "causal-comparative" of 'ex post facto'" (observing something and then looking for causes), "true experimental" (see below on treatment effects),

13

"quasi-experimental" (see below on treatment effects as well as Campbell & Stanley, 1963), and "action." "Action" research is the type that has been used in many D. Min. studies. It involves implementing a program to see if it works. It is the weakest of the nine types Isaac and Michael discuss.

This list of forms of research might help you crystalize your approach to your project. Some of these are particularly appropriate for program evaluation, and we introduce them in the next three sections of this chapter.

Incidentally, the Handbook in Research and Evaluation by Isaac and Michael (1981) is a compact and useful survey of many topics related to thesis research.

Treatment Effects

In general, empirical research can be divided into two categories: experiment and simple observation. As with most simple distinctions, this breaks down on closer observation (see Campbell & Stanley, 1963), but the simple distinction will serve us well.

"Experimentation" involves attempting to cause something to happen. This is done by matching several groups and doing something different with each of them. Another approach is to start with different groups (in which you can specify what the differences are) and doing the same thing to them. In both cases, you then compare the results. "Simple observation" involves observing what happens in a single group. Surveys and case studies are two approaches to simple observation.

Clingan (1978) did a D. Min. project that, for our purposes, would be classified as experimental. He developed a 12-week small group experience for older people in the church and a one-day retreat for a similar group of people. Both the 12-week class and the one-day retreat had the same goals. He then formulated and tested hypotheses about the over-all effect of the experiences and how the two groups would compare. (In general, the 12-week class was "better.")

14

Control Groups

The key to treatment effects studies is the concept of "control." We may do something with a group of people and notice that it is followed by some observed quality. If that quality was not characteristic of the group before the "treatment," we may argue that whatever we did caused the quality to develop. But maybe it would have developed anyway.

The best way to check this is with a "control group." In its pure form, the control group is subject to all the influences that affect the treatment group, except that the control group does not receive the treatment. In diagram form, the study looks like Figure 2-1.

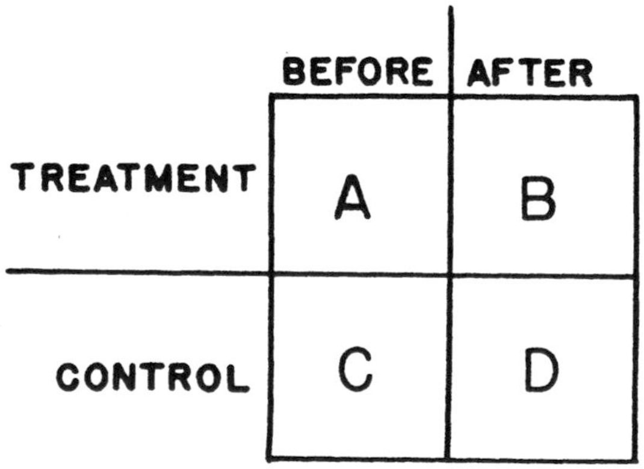

	BEFORE	AFTER
TREATMENT	A	B
CONTROL	C	D

Figure 2-1. Typical research design including a control group.

If "b" is larger than "a," and "d" is not larger than "c," we can say the treatment was responsible for the change.

Pure control groups exist only in the laboratory. Probably no D. Min. project will be "well controlled," but this does not invalidate the concept.

In Clingan's study, mentioned above, the two

15

treatment groups, in a certain sense, serve as controls for each other. In some cases, you can approximate a control group by applying your outcome measurements to people who are somewhat similar to the treatment group, such as members of another church, or even other people in the community.

The basic question posed by the concept of "control" is, "How can you be sure that what you did caused the effect?" Keep this question in mind. If, as you plan your project, you have trouble answering it, read further in works such as Kerlinger (1973) and Campbell and Stanley (1963).

Time Series

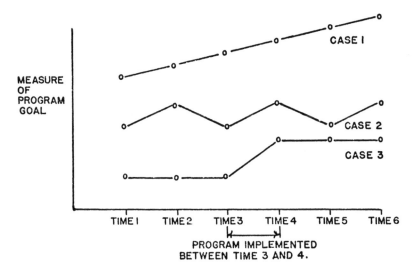

Figure 2-2.   Three possible outcomes from a "Time Series" Study. *Note. Carol H. Weiss, Evaluation Research: Methods of Assessing Program Effectiveness, Copyright 1972, p.68. Adapted by permission of Prentice-Hall,Inc., Englewood Cliffs, NJ.

16

If the focus of your study is the institution, one useful way to "control" your observations is to observe the institution over a period of time, and do the treatment in the "middle" of the observations. If the observations show either a consistent trend, or no trend at all, you cannot claim the treatment was effective. If the observations show the group as static before the treatment, you may have a good argument for treatment effectiveness. An idealized representation of this is shown in Figure 2-2. The change can be attributed to the treatment only in case 3.

This approach to research is most useful when you have records of the key variables, such as church attendance, church membership, offerings, budget category expenditures, or anything else on which records are kept routinely.

An Example of Treatment Effects Research

As an example of treatment effects research, consider "Effects of a Death Education Program Upon Secondary School Students." It demonstrates a typical design for such research. The fact that the experiment was not successful is also instructive. It is quite possible that your project will not accomplish what you had hoped.

Bailis and Kennedy (1977) taught equivalent courses (although one lasted six weeks and the other nine weeks) to students in two high schools, one in a small town, the other in a suburb. In each case, another class, not studying death education, was selected as a control. All students were tested before and after the course. The research design looked like Figure 2-3.

Two tests were used, the "Fear of Death Scale" (FOD), and the "Death Anxiety Scale" (DAS). After the final testing, statistical analysis showed no significant differences between the two schools, so the two treatment groups and the two control groups were combined, as shown in Figure 2-4. The entries in Figure 2-4 show the mean (average) scores on the two tests. scores on FOD can range from +3 (strong fear) to -3 (no fear), and scores on DAS range from 0 (no

17

anxiety) to 15 (a great deal of anxiety).

		BEFORE	AFTER
SCHOOL 1	TREATMENT (36 STUDENTS)		
	CONTROL (18 STUDENTS)		
SCHOOL 2	TREATMENT (15 STUDENTS)		
	CONTROL (13 STUDENTS)		

Figure 2-3. Original design for Death
Education Study.

	BEFORE	AFTER
TREATMENT (51 STUDENTS)	FOD = .13 DAS = 8.3	FOD = .41 DAS = 7.9
CONTROL (31 STUDENTS)	FOD = .22 DAS = 8.6	FOD = .23 DAS = 7.9

Figure 2-4. Summary results from Death
Education Study.

18

The results of this study are fairly typical of such efforts (including study courses taught in the church) regardless of subject matter. We note several things:

(1) The FOD shows a statistically significant difference between the "before" and "after" scores of those students who took the course. If there were no control group, whose scores are between the "before" and "after" of the treatment group, we might over-emphasize the treatment results. (Bailis and Kennedy over-emphasize them as it is.)

(2) The second measure (DAS), which essentially does not change, provides another corrective.

(3) Knowing the range of the two tests, we can say that students were essentially neutral about death, both before and after the course.

(4) To the degree that there was an effect, it was the opposite of the teachers' intention. The students feared death more at the end than at the beginning.

Was the effort in teaching this course worthwhile? I would like to think so, even though its value didn't show up in the testing, but this is nothing other than a prejudice. We must say clearly that we do not know what changes the course brought about. Though negative, this is a stronger conclusion than one sometimes finds in D. Min. theses where the student tries to justify the unjustifiable on the basis of personal feeling. In this case, at least we know where not to look for changes in attitude toward death resulting from a short death education course.

A Suggestion

The study of treatment effects can involve very sophisticated methodological problems, and if you find yourself doing this sort of project, consult with someone with psychological, sociological, or educational research expertise at a local university before trying to perform the treatment and collect information.

Survey Research

At its simplest, survey research is the basic counting and tabulation of opinions, knowledge, and objective facts. Frequently, such information is precisely what you need to make decisions.

The survey research project involves four methodological concerns: questionnaire design, sampling, adequate questionnaire return, and data analysis.

Chapter 7 deals with some of the basic problems of questionnaire design, but it is appropriate at this point to say that your questionnaire will be only as good as your understanding of what you want to find out. When your project is adequately defined, you can write a questionnaire that will give you the information you need without wasting the respondent's time.

Plan to spend time designing, testing, and refining your questionnaire, because it is the heart of any survey project. Don't overlook how others have dealt with similar topics. You may find that someone else has asked a certain question in just the right way as a part of a previous research project.

You should also plan to spend time, effort, and expense on getting the completed questionnaires back. This may mean postage, phone calls and visits. Follow-up mailings should be part of your initial plans.

As you design your questionnaire, you should have a definite plan for analyzing the information it yields. Lists of percentage response to each item are often misleading. Are there differences among groups? Compare men and women, age groupings, groupings by levels of education, degree of activity in the church, or any other groupings that might yield interesting

20

and useful differences.

Survey Sampling

It may be possible for you to ask "everyone" to complete the questionnaire, such as when your research is limited to your congregation, and you can ask everyone who is a member to respond. If so, and if, through home visitations, you can get everyone to respond, sampling will not be a concern. Strictly speaking, if you ignore sampling, you must also assume that your only concern is with the group of people who respond, and you have no intention of generalizing your results beyond them to other groups of people.

More likely, you will not be able to ask for, much less get, 100% response, and you would at least want to generalize your results to other congregations you might serve during your life. So you have to ask who is represented by the people who completed the questionnaire. If your survey is in your church, are they people who particularly appreciate your ministry, or do they have an above average desire that you change your style of ministry? Are regular participants over-represented in the sample? Is any age or occupation group or level of education over-represented? If you are distributing your questionnaire within the wider community, there are even more variables to cause concern.

The dangers of improper sampling are illustrated by the Literary Digest presidential election survey in 1936. Literary Digest polled ten million people, and predicted that Alf Landon would win the election. Instead, Roosevelt won, and some say that the resulting loss of credibility of the Literary Digest caused the magazine to fold. What went wrong? The poll was conducted over the telephone and through the magazine, and only the affluent had telephones and magazine subscriptions. The sample was biased (Simon, 1969, pp. 111-115).

Since then, the theory and practice of sampling has become quite sophisticated, and public opinion polls by Gallup, Harris, and similar professionals are usually amazingly accurate.

For your purposes, sampling need not be the major focus of your research, but you need to attend to three questions:

(1) How is your sample drawn, randomly, or otherwise?

(2) What is the profile of your sample (age, sex, education, etc.)?

(3) What is the profile of those who failed to return the questionnaire?

How to Select a Random Sample

In general, a random sample will give you the best possible representation of a group. Although it is not always possible to have a random sample, samples should be random whenever possible. To draw a random sample, obtain a table of random numbers (see the appendix of almost any statistics textbook), and write a rule for making the selection.

For example, suppose I want to draw a random sample of 50 names from my church directory. The directory has seven pages of names, with three columns per page and a maximum of 15 names per column. A possible rule would read:

Enter the table of random numbers at a randomly selected point, and use the next four digits. (a) The first digit will indicate the page number (1-7), unless it is 8, 9, or 0. In that case, use the next digit that is not 8, 9, or 0. (b) The digit after that will indicate the column, with 1, 4, or 7, indicating column one, 2, 5, or 8, indicating column two, and 3, 6, or 9, indicating column three. If the digit is 0, proceed to the next non-0 digit. (c) The next two digits will indicate the name in the column, with the top name being indicated by 01, 16, 31, 46, 61, or 76, the second name indicated by 02, 17, 32, 47, 62, or 77, and so on, with the 15th name indicated by 15, 30, 45, 60, 75, or 90. If the two digits in the table are

22

91 through 99, or 00, proceed to the following pair of digits. If there are fewer than 15 names in the column, and there is no name to match the indicated number, proceed to the next pair of digits.

This is not the only acceptable rule for selecting this sample. The point is to devise a method to retain the random quality of your sample. As you can see, such rules can become complex, and it may help to "flow chart" them, as in Figure 2-5.

Other Questions

Once you have drawn your sample, use your "common sense" in looking at it. Is it obviously unrepresentative in any way? If you used a random method of selecting it, the odds are against its being unrepresentative, but it may happen.

Finally, when you have coaxed completed questionnaires out of as many people as possible, try to find out something about those people who did not complete them. Is there anything about those people as a group that makes them different from the group that completed the questionnaire? This analysis will give you a good clue toward interpreting how valid your questionnaire responses are.

If you plan a large survey, read more about sampling techniques, and if possible, consult with a sociologist in your seminary or at a local university. Every survey presents its own problems, and in a large survey, the problems can be quite sophisticated.

Data Analysis

If you discover differences between groups, don't call them different until you have tested them for significance. "Significance" is a technical term that refers to the stability of the difference throughout the population (see Chapter 9).

In addition to looking for group differences, you should plan to check correlations. "Correlation" is a

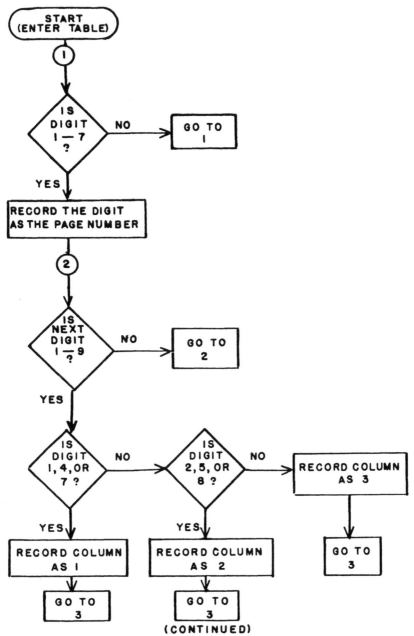

Figure 2-5. Drawing a random sample
from a church directory.

24

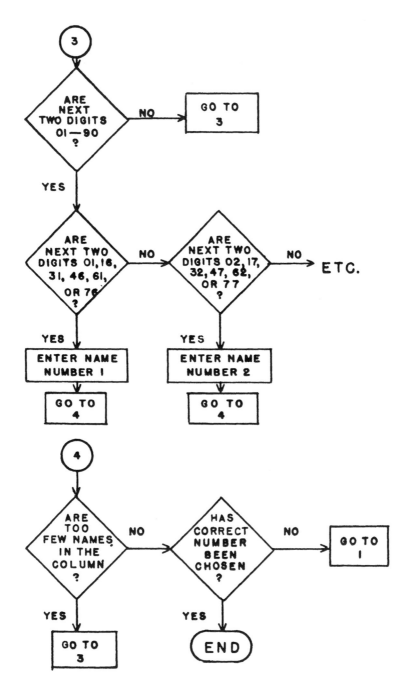

measure of the relationship between two responses on the survey (see Chapter 9 and the following section). In addition, you may find other techniques of statistical analysis useful. We will introduce some of them later in this book.

If you find yourself planning a survey research project, you may want to read the article by Schroeder (1977).

Example of Correlation in Survey Research

In a study of influences on vocational commitment of Protestant ministers in the Chicago area (Hoge, Dyble & Polk, 1981), 667 usable questionnaires were returned (a 61% response rate) from seven denominations. Percentage responses (p. 138) showed that over three - quarters of the ministers had a strong commitment to the ministry. Such information is not very interesting, and it has limited use. It is more interesting to relate the expressed vocational commitment of the ministers to other things, such as how much mobility they have, how well they are paid, how well they get along with their congregation, whether their family shares their commitment, and how challenging the present pastorate is.

The authors calculated such correlations, and made the interesting discovery that "challenge" seems to be the most important factor related to a minister's vocational commitment. The question, "To what extent is your present position challenging and absorbing?" correlated .57 with commitment to the present pastorate and .41 with general commitment to the ministry (p. 140). These figures are not only statistically significant, but are large enough to be of interest. In contrast, the pastor's judgement as to whether he or she was well paid or under paid showed a low correlation of .18 with commitment to the present pastorate and .19 with commitment to the ministry. As a matter of fact, all correlations are low, except for those having to do with challenge. Clearly, perceived challenge is a very important factor in commitment to the ministry, an interesting and important finding.

Case Studies

Case studies, also called field studies, are descriptions of phenomena, such as groups, events, classes, and institutions. According to Isaac and Michael (1981, p. 48), "case studies are in-depth investigations of a given social unit resulting in a complete, well-organized picture of that unit."

If you are planning a case study, you should focus on the specification of "well-organized." The case study is a tempting approach to D. Min. research, because it appears to require a minimum of planning. The temptation is to do something in the parish, such as start a series of neighborhood groups, a summer neighborhood youth program, or a church/community task force on some social problem. At the end of the project write a narrative about how the project was conceived, organized, developed, and how it turned out. Include a chapter of subjective evaluation, perhaps buttressed by evaluation response forms from the participants, and call it a thesis.

The result is difficult to read, because of its strict chronological organization, and not particularly useful to others because of its loose evaluation.

It is almost impossible to conceive of a parish project that has not been done before and described in writing. If you are certain that your project should be written as a case study, do a careful literature review, and make a chart of how similar projects have been organized. Chart the strengths and weaknesses of the projects you review. Talk with other pastors, too, and see if they have been involved in similar projects. What pitfalls did they find? What improvements can they suggest?

With your project well thought out, identify a framework for observation. What elements of the project will you observe?

Example of a Model: Communication

If possible, relate your case study to a theoretical model. A model is a specification of

27

variables that are important in a setting, and how
these variables are related to one another. The model
may simply specify the type of relationship (such as a
sequential relationship), or may loosely specify the
relative strengths of relationship. It may even
specify relationships precisely in terms of
mathematical formulas.

One example of a model is the Shannon-Weaver
model of communication (Figure 2-6), which considers
the sender, message encoding, the channel, noise,
message decoding, the receiver, and feedback as
crucial elements of communication. If your project is
a case study primarily concerned with communication,
you should select this or some other model of
communication and organize your thesis so it deals
with the elements of the model you have selected.

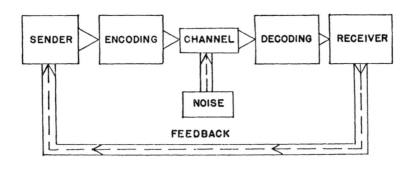

Figure 2-6. Communication Model
(After Shannon & Weaver)

Example of a Model: Innovation

For another example, the theory of innovation and
change suggests that when people accept or reject a
new idea or way of doing things, they go through
several stages. Various authors describe them in
slightly different ways (Havelock, 1971, Chapter 10),
but Rogers' (1962) list is typical: (a) awareness,
(b) interest, (c) evaluation, (d) trial, (e) adoption

28

(or rejection). If your project can be seen as an attempt to introduce a new idea and have it accepted, and your approach is a case study, you will probably want to watch for this sequence of responses.

Innovation research also suggests that a given person is likely to respond to any innovation in about the same way as that person responds to any other innovation (cf. Rogers, 1962, p. 162). "Innovators" are those two or three percent of the population who will "try anything." Their opinions carry little weight in the community. "Early adoptors" are about 15% of the population. They adopt new ideas after serious thought, and they tend to be opinion leaders. The "early majority" and "late majority" constitute about two-thirds of the population, and when they adopt the innovation, it is firmly fixed in the community. However, there remains a group of about 15% of the community who are very slow to change. They have been called "laggards," although some researchers have argued against the use of such a pejorative term. Rogers related these groups to the so-called "normal curve," but perhaps the model is clearer as presented by Havelock, Figure 2-7.

Innovation theory is well developed, and includes many other features. Here we have presented only enough to illustrate how a model can be the basis of a case study.

Example of a Model: Ministry

A less well developed example is found in Peck (1983). She discusses the possibility of developing "a model of ministry focused on the three interrelated elements of personhood, community and global society" (p. 94). She refers to three empirical studies to help define these elements. All three studies spoke of the value of churches responding simultaneously to the needs of individuals and to the wider community. Such churches are stronger than those that involve a single focus.

Peck suggests ways that each of the three foci might be manifested in the congregation. A case study taking this model as a point of reference would look

29

for these foci, try to describe their
interrelationships, and possibly try to modify them.

Objective Observation

How will you observe what you report about? You
should certainly have more than your own subjective
observation as a basis for your writing. You may want
to call on one or more independent observers. Perhaps
there is someone in your congregation who is not
directly involved in the project and who is a
qualified observer. Perhaps a neighbor pastor can
help you observe. Perhaps a denominational executive
can help you.

You will probably also want to develop some
response forms (questionnaires or "tests") to help you
see how people involved in the project feel about it
at different points. You will want to have an
evaluation procedure clearly in mind before you start
the project. What do you expect to happen at the end
of the project? How will you know how well it
happened, or if it happened at all?

Consider Alternatives

A great deal of planning goes into a case study,
but once you have done the planning, there is one more
thing to do before you start the project. Review your
plans carefully, asking whether the case study is the
best approach to your project. Could you test the
same research question with more conclusive results if
your project involved treatment effects? For example,
if you have in mind developing a course of instruction
to help people appreciate their denominational
heritage, you might ask if they would develop an equal
appreciation of their denominational heritage if each
sermon over a period of time included one illustration
drawn from the denominational heritage.

Simply teaching the course and observing the
process would result in what we are calling a case
study. Comparing sermon illustrations with the course
would be what we have called a "treatment effects"
study. How could it be done? Preach the sermons to

30

your own congregation, and arrange to teach the course
in another congregation.

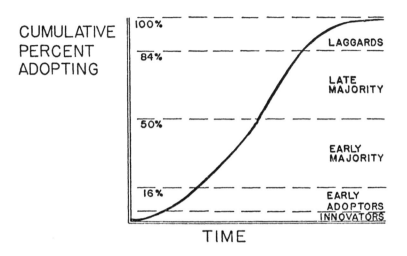

CUMULATIVE
PERCENT
ADOPTING

100%

84%

LAGGARDS

LATE
MAJORITY

50%

EARLY
MAJORITY

16%

EARLY
ADOPTORS
INNOVATORS

TIME

Figure 2-7.   Innovation adoption as a function
of time.

One More Example of Program Evaluation:
Analyzing Some Worship Preferences

In 1982, the Division on Evangelism of the United
Methodist South Indiana Annual Conference decided that
it would be appropriate to survey laity on their
attitudes toward worship.

They distributed a questionnaire to lay delegates
to the 1982 Annual Conference session. Annual Conference is a four day business meeting, so lay delegates
have several non-typical characteristics. They are
leaders, and more active in their congregations than
most members. They probably understand the
organizational life of the church better than most
members, and this may be the focus of their
commitment, while other church members may focus their
commitment on learning, charitable service,

31

fellowship, prayer, etc. Lay delegates are also free to attend the four day Annual conference. The practical consequence of this is that a large number of lay delegates are retired.

None of this destroys the value of the questionnaire responses, but it is invalid to interpret any survey or test responses apart from an understanding of who provided them.

One of the questions was, "What are you seeking most when you attend a worship service?" People were given a set of 20 "purposes," and asked to rank the ten most important, a score of 10 being the highest priority. The results are shown in Table 2-1, which uses "size of church" as an independent variable.

Such a table can have several uses. The Division of Evangelism hoped it would be used as the basis of discussion. As they said:

> We wish we knew what people meant when they checked "God's Presence" or "Inspiration." While music was very important to some persons, there are undoubtably many different opinions about what kind of music is meaningful.
>
> The ranking is helpful to get a broad view of attitudes. Many more questions need to be asked in order to know what underlies these responses. We urge classes and groups in the local church to dig more deeply into these questions. What do persons seek in your church? Do we need to help persons turn their hopes and desires (their seeking) to some new areas? How can pastors be helped and set free to lead more effectively through worship?

For a purpose such as this, Table 2-1 is appropriate. It makes no difference that the responses came from older people with a special interest in church organization, and it does not matter whether the differences are statistically significant or not. A youth group, a young married class, or a ladies' society can use the table as a spring-board for discussing their own feelings.

Table 2-1

Ranking of Aspects of Worship
in Various Size Churches

	OVERALL	UNDER 50	50-100	100-150	150-250	OVER 250
God's Presence	8.03	8.1	8.4	8.6	7.8	8.4
Inspiration	5.85	5.6	6.4	5.9	5.2	5.8
Spiritual Fulfillment	5.36	4.7	5.3	6.9	5.5	5.1
Fellowship	3.76	3.5	3.0	4.1	4.2	4.6
Strength	3.34	3.6	2.9	4.6	3.1	3.0
Guidance	3.28	4.1	3.9	3.0	3.1	3.6
Challenge	3.13	3.2	3.7	2.2	4.0	3.3
Love	3.08	3.3	3.6	2.9	3.3	2.9
Music	2.50	3.0	2.4	3.2	2.4	3.3
Bible Study	2.23	2.1	2.2	2.0	2.8	2.0
Forgiveness	2.19	1.9	2.5	2.8	2.4	1.6
Peace	2.03	2.0	2.4	2.2	2.0	1.8
Joy	1.93	2.8	2.0	1.6	1.6	2.2
Hope	1.83	2.7	1.3	1.3	2.6	2.2
Celebration	1.69	.9	1.7	1.5	2.3	2.3
Comfort	.92	1.1	1.3	1.4	1.1	.4
How-to's	.50	.9	.5	.3	1.1	.5
Excitement	.34	.0	.4	.1	.0	.8
Sponteneity	.21	.6	.4	.1	.0	.0
Variety	.19	.1	.1	.2	.1	.4

*Note. From "The Green Sheet," Division of Evangelism, United Methodist South Indiana Annual Conference, 1982.

A pastor might find it valuable to do a D. Min. study around such discussions. For example, tape record such discussions among every organized group in the church, do a content analysis of each discussion, compare them, and draw conclusions for redesigning the worship service. After using the new worship format for a while, survey the congregation to find out whether they see it as an improvement.

Another use for information similar to that in Table 2-1, is as a basis for making administrative

33

decisions. In our everyday work, we cannot conduct a church-wide discussion program related to every decision, yet we sometimes want to base our decisions on more than a personal hunch. We look to the questionnaire as an efficient way of getting the information we seek.

If we were to make decisions based on Table 2-1, at a minimum we would want to consider the special qualities of the people who completed the questionnaire, and we would want to know how many people in each category returned questionnaires. In most cases, we would want to know if differences were statistically significant, and we might want to know what the standard deviations of the mean scores were. (We will deal with these issues in later chapters. Such considerations would probably not be too important in interpreting Table 2-1.)

Then we would look at what people seek from worship. We can roughly categorize these into three groups: Those which are not subject to administrative control, those which are somewhat subject to our decisionmaking, and those over which we can definitely make decisions. For example, "God's presence" is certainly beyond our control, and "inspiration" and "spiritual fulfillment" are also probably in this category. (Of course it is possible to destroy the atmosphere of worship by saying and doing highly inappropriate things, but that is beside the point.) We can clearly make decisions about such things as music and Bible study. We can exercise some control over such things as "fellowship," "guidance" and "challenge."

Given such a list, we make decisions where we can, and after a period of time, check to see if our decisions had the results we intended.

A third use of something like Table 2-1 is to raise questions for further research. There is a tendency for those categories over which we have the most control to be least important. For example, it is fairly easy to add variety to worship, but in this survey, variety had the lowest priority. If the pastor has some responsibility for the quality of worship, then it is appropriate to ask, "Under what circumstances do worshippers feel a sense of God's presence, or inspired, or spiritually fulfilled, or a

34

sense of fellowship or strength?"

It is almost certain that any data will raise additional questions, whether these questions are an extension of your study, or are left for future studies.

CHAPTER III

WHAT DO I WANT TO FIND OUT?
FRAMING THE QUESTION

The Nature of the Question

Your D. Min. thesis should have one primary goal: to help you become a better minister. If it does not do that, it is a waste of your time, a waste of the examining committee's time, and a waste of time for anyone who happens to read it at a later date. The thesis may not be an outstanding piece of research and writing, but the process of considering the issues and working with them in the life of the parish should change your life.

This suggests that your thesis project should not be a report of the implementation of some church program that you would have initiated in any case. It should, in some sense, be a new approach to ministry.

"New" does not mean "original," but new to you. Through the project, you should gain new insights and skills, or answer old questions. Originality of research is a standard for academic doctoral programs, such as the Ph.D. The standards for the professional doctorate should be no less rigorous, but the thesis should be "skill producing," rather than "knowledge producing." It is quite possible that the most professionally helpful project for you will be a replication of a study that has been done before. If that's the case, try to do it better than it's been done before.

Context of the Question:
Ministry and the Life of the Church

A D. Min. project may be rooted in any seminary field of study, but it will be related to the practice of ministry. Because of this, at an early point in thinking about the question, you should think about the structure of ministry. What aspects of ministry hold the greatest interest for you?

In an early stage of their research, the authors of Ministry in America (Schuller, Strommen & Brekke, 1980) developed the following taxonomy which might help you focus on an area for a D. Min. project (p. 557):

I. The Minister in a Profession
   A. The Human Side of the Profession
   B. The Realm of Ideas
   C. Religious Commitment
   D. Clergy as Theologians

II. The Minister as a Person
   A. Stability of Spirit and Attitude
   B. Positive Spirit
   C. Psychologically Free to Serve Others
   D. Alert and Open to New Possibilities
   E. Able to Live and Act as an Autonomous Person
   F. An Exemplar

III. The Minister as a Skilled Leader
   A. Skilled in Relating to People
   B. Skilled in Conflict Resolution
   C. Skilled Leader of Group Discussion
   D. Skilled Administrator in Effecting Change
   E. Skilled as Trainer, Educator, and Theologian in Developing the Resources of People
   F. Skilled in Encouraging Mutuality
   G. Skilled as a Manager

IV. The Minister in Professional Roles
   A. Leader of Public Worship
   B. Community Leader
   C. Prophet
   D. Preacher
   E. Evangelist
   F. Educator
   G. Counselor
   H. Ecumenical Leader

This taxonomy was developed as a basis for cataloging a collection of 1,200 ministerial qualities the research team had collected. From that point, the Ministry in America study surveyed clergy and laity to see what qualities are perceived to be most important (and what qualities are perceived to be harmful). At some point in preparation for your project, you may

38

find it useful to study Ministry in America.

At this point, however, you can use the taxonomy to help you identify those aspects of ministry that most interest you, or where you have the most persistent questions. Your project might best be in one of these areas.

In a study similar to the Ministry in America study, though much more limited, Haburn (1976) surveyed 188 ministers of the General Association of Regular Baptist churches and the Conservative Baptist Association of America about the competencies required for ministry. He reported the following structure:

I. Administration
   A. Program Development
   B. Program Operation
   C. Community Relations
   D. Counseling

II. Leadership
   A. Individual Ability
   B. Interpersonal Relations

III. Management
   A. Human Resources
   B. Financial Resources

Both of these research projects focused on the ministry, more than on the life of the church. A D. Min. project may also focus on the sociology of the congregation ("church growth" projects would be an example), or on psychological aspects of the congregation, rather than on the work of the minister. But if you focus on the ministry, these two outlines may help you refine your goal.

The point is, even if your greatest desire is that your project grow out of the Oracles of Balaam (Numbers 22-24, etc.), decide how it will relate to the ministry and the life of the church.

Building a Question

Observe Something

To do a D. Min. project, you must observe something. This will be true no matter whether the project is an exercise in teaching, a case study, or any other sort of project.

So if you don't have a question, start building one by deciding what you want to observe. Start by identifying it without asking questions. You can observe pastoral calling, pre-marital counseling, preaching, mission offerings, clergy tenure, the history of the congregation, congregational attitudes toward war, church utility bills. . .

Simply identify something that interests you.

Have a Frame of Reference

A pastor, denominational executive and lay person will not see an event in the life of the church in the same way. A pastor and assistant pastor will also have different perspectives, and different pastors emphasize different things in their ministry.

To what degree are you authoritarian in your ministry? To what degree are you collegial? To what degree do you emphasize ministry of the laity?

What are your priorities among ministerial activities? Three ministers who find their greatest fulfillment respectively in teaching, program planning, and pastoral counseling may have equal regard for the youth program of the church, but their work with the youth will be quite different. Each of them should understand their own perspective before doing a D. Min. project on youth work.

Formulate Objectives and Hypotheses

Now you can start framing your question. Why are

you going to observe what you have decided to observe? The answer will be an objective. What do you expect to see? The answer will be a hypothesis.

State the objectives and hypotheses as specifically as you can, and when you write your paper, write them in an early chapter with as much explanation as necessary. They will both guide your research and help the reader understand your research.

As you write your objectives, number them so that they stand out and you cannot ignore them. Consider the following paragraphs from a D. Min. thesis (Flannery, 1976, pp. 32-33):

> The project is called a "Bible Skills Workshop" to distinguish it from Bible study. It is not a theological study of the contents of the Bible, nor is it a workshop to help teachers learn how to teach the Bible to children. The purpose of the workshop is to provide church school teachers, as well as other adults, with some basic information about the Bible, and to introduce them to the tools which will aid them in Bible study.
>
> . . .
>
> Most of the workshops which I have designed require special training equipment and are, therefore, workshops which I personally conduct for groups of churches in the associations. This workshop, on the other hand, is designed to be used by the pastor with the members of his own congregation. I had church school teachers primarily in mind in developing the workshop, but it need not be limited to that group. It can very well be part of confirmation instruction, a special series for adults, or a program for other groups or organizations in the church.
>
> It is my hope that the workshop will enrich the understanding and deepen the appreciation of the Bible as a book for use in the church's educational program.

41

I agree with Miller that "In its
teaching-learning situations the church
must raise the Bible to the central and
crucial place above all else that is
regarded as important to teach." If the
workshop provides teachers with the
stimulation to further study and acquaints
them with the basic tools for creative
Bible study and teaching, it will have
achieved its purpose.

Flannery did some good work on his thesis. The
suggestion here is that his project would have been
even better if the objectives had been isolated and
analyzed, rather than being imbedded in a narrative.
Here is one way to re-state the objectives in these
three paragraphs:

The project is to design a workshop which
(1) will teach basic information about
the Bible and teach about tools which
will aid Bible study.

(2) can be used effectively by a pastor
working with members of his or her
congregation.

(3) will enrich understanding and deepen
appreciation of the Bible as a book
for use in the church's educational
program.

(4) will stimulate teachers to further
creative Bible study.

Objectives that are stated this explicitly can
then be refined. Do they say more or less than you
intended them to say? What are the elements that need
to be defined? (We will say more about this in
Chapter 6.) For example, what is "basic information"
in objective 1? What is "effective use" in objective
2? What are "appreciation" and "understanding" in
objective 3? What is "creative Bible study" in
objective 4?

Mager (1962) writes about "behavioral objectives"
and sets forth some stringent requirements for stating
them. You will not necessarily be writing behavioral
objectives, but his rules are worth thinking about in

42

any case. An objective should state:

(1) what is to be done.

(2) the conditions under which it will be done.

(3) the degree to which it will be done.

Given these three criteria, we can consider the four objectives above as parts of one larger objective. 1, 3, and 4 state what is to be done. 2 states the conditions. There is no indication of how well these things will be done. The question of "degree" will depend in part on the definitions of "basic information," "effective use," and such.

Strictly speaking, "hypotheses" refer to the anticipated result when several treatments (such as two approaches to Bible study) are compared. In a study such as Flannery's, the design and testing of a training program, we can sensibly speak of a statement such as, "teachers will show evidence of continued Bible study six months after the course," as a hypothesis. A good hypothesis will imply a way of evaluating the outcome of the project.

Identify Variables

Every situation involves variables. For example, if you change one person in a small group, the group will be different. Chapter 6 will be concerned with variables, but at this point it should be said that one step in refining your question is identifying the key variables.

The situation you plan to observe would be different if certain features of the situation were different. What are those features? How much control do you have over those features? If you have a clear perception of what the variables are, framing the question will be greatly simplified.

Evaluation

Build evaluation procedures into your question

from the beginning. This will be a statement of exactly what you are going to observe, how you are going to observe it (tests, questionnaires, third party reports, your own subjective observation, etc.), and what results will indicate success or failure.

As we said above, if you have hypotheses, they will imply evaluation procedures. For example, Clingan (1978, p. 13), gave the following as one of his hypotheses, along with a statement of how it would be tested:

> 2. A one-day retreat for older adults sponsored by a region of the church cannot have as great an impact on the lives of the participants as can a 12-week small "life enrichment" group of older adults held within the life of a church congregation. . .
>
> Tested in both one-day older adult retreats and a 12-week small group experience setting. By comparing the impact of the retreats as compared to the small group experience through the measurements of all the instruments applicable to the two settings, we are in a position to determine whether this hypothesis moves toward being accepted or rejected.

It is not absolutely necessary to state formal hypotheses, and sometimes it is not even appropriate to state them. But you need to consider evaluation procedures from the beginning of the project. Williams (1971?, p. 19) provides this example:

> Earlier in the paper, I stated that the objectives of the project were:
> 1. To provide clergymen with a desire to be involved in mental health training programs and skills.
>
> 2. To equip clergymen with skills that will be helpful to them in working with their communities in the area of mental health.
>
> 3. To develop in clergymen the desire

to change from their present
functioning so that they can
be more useful to the total
community.

I would now like to state subobjectives
[sic] under that heading. It is hoped that
from the skills they have learned, they
will find themselves more involved in the
area of divorce, marital, individual
counseling and premarital sexual counseling
within their communities. It is also hoped
that because of the interest change in the
clergymen, they will find themselves
involved in consultation with colleagues,
doctors and families about the functioning
of persons within their communities. If
the changes have taken place, and if their
involvement in certain types of counseling
has increased, then the project has been
successful, and the skills have been
helpful.

Williams used a questionnaire at the beginning
and end of the project to test the variables he
mentions.

The "How Do I . . . . " Question

It is neither unusual nor inappropriate for the
minister to approach the D. Min. thesis with a
"program" orientation. The consequence of this
orientation is to phrase the question with the words,
"How do I . . . ?" or "How can I . . . ?" The
problem is that this is not a question that will lead
to growth in the ministry. By itself, such a question
leads the minister to plan a church program similar to
any other program he or she has planned in the past.
It may be more elaborate, or more study may have gone
into it, but it will not be qualitatively different.

If you are stuck on a "How do I . . . ?"
question, go back to the above discussion of "building
a question." If "How do I . . . ?" remains the most
important question in your ministry, try to revise it
so that it deals with some clear options. Try asking
a question of the form, "Would approach 'A' or approach

45

'B' be more effective in solving this problem in my congregation?" You might also ask, "How have my peers solved (or tried to solve) this problem in their congregations?"

If this doesn't work, and you still ask "How do I . . . ?" then approach the project as a case study (see Chapter 2), and give much thought to how you should evaluate the project. Otherwise you will never know whether you developed a way to "do it" or not.

Background Reading for Framing the Question

The question may come from a program of reading. Chapter 5 gives examples of how questions might be developed from theological books and articles.

In addition, you may want to skim some of the sociological studies of religion (and don't neglect the older ones). These will suggest comparisons between the data collected as much as several decades ago and the people of your congregation or community. In keeping with the professional focus of the D. Min. program, you would select comparisons that have implications for pastoral work.

For example, Religious Beliefs of Youth (Ross, 1950) is a 250 page report of a study conducted in 1949-1950. The people surveyed were YMCA constituents between the ages of 18 and 29. It involved questionnaire responses from 1,935 people and interviews with 100 people. For the most part the study was well done,* and it is carefully reported. One thought-provoking note from the book is that anal-

---

* Well done, but not perfect. In Chapter 7, we will note how some of the questionnaire items could have been improved. Also, statistical analysis is extremely limited, partly, no doubt, because all statistical analysis at that time had to be done without aid of computers. At points, the presentation would have been improved if correlation coefficients had been reported. The critical student will also be interested in comparing the content analysis of the interviews with current standards for content analysis.

46

ysis of 75 interviews in which prayer was discussed suggested four categories (p. 64): "(1) those for whom prayer seems to be a meaningful way of communication with God." (17%) "(2) those for whom prayer approximates a period of self analysis or meditation." (26%) "(3) those for whom prayer is a kind of technique (a kind of magical gesture) which can be used in time of crisis or need." (42%) "(4) those who never pray." (15%). The report gives sample quotations from the interviews as well as questionnaire responses on prayer from the larger sample.

The questions suggested by this information are, "Can the same attitudes toward prayer be found in my church?" "What percentage of people in my church hold various attitudes toward prayer related to other variables, such as frequency of attendance at worship?"

The Religious Beliefs of Youth study serves as a starter, suggesting these questions for the thesis. The actual project should begin with a theological study of prayer which might suggest refinements or additional questions. When the study is finished, the data will have implications for preaching, teaching and counseling.

Families in the Church (Fairchild and Wynn, 1961) is a study of approximately 1,000 Presbyterians from across the U.S. Most of the information is from group interview, so it is primarily qualitative rather than quantitative.* Here is one of many conclusions that might spark a D. Min. project:

> . . . . today's Protestant families do only a minimum of worship as family groups, refer all too seldom to their church literature on the Christian family, and tend to a vagueness in theological understanding that pervades their household conversation and common life.

The one family subject that receives more

---

* This book begins with a theological study of the family, followed by empirical research. Because of this, it would make a good model for a D. Min. thesis.

47

pulpit attention than any other is family worship. This traditional ideal of Protestant families gathered together for Christian worship has been handed down from generation to generation in sermons and church literature. Whether the households actually preserve the tradition from generation to generation is more open to question. Extolled in thousands of magazine articles, sermons, and references every year, regular worship in the home was seldom found among the families we surveyed. (p. 184)

Is this a theme of your preaching? If so, is it effective? Can you research some alternative plans for making it effective?

The Fragmented Layman (Campbell & Fukuyama, 1970) is a survey of 8,000 plus members of the United Church of Christ. The complete questionnaire with responses is included in an appendix. Many of the questionnaire items suggest D. Min. projects. For example, item 21, "As far as you know, how much time does your minister spend on each of the activities listed below?" and item 22, "For each of the same list of activities, check whether you think your minister spends too much, too little, or about the right amount of time," suggests studying these same perceptions in your congregation and negotiating a job description. By the way, if your question happens to involve lay perceptions of pastoral roles, you will want to read pages 180-184 in Families in the Church, as well as Ministry in America (Schuller, Strommen & Brekke, 1980).

There are many such sociological studies that might help you. Among them are Espy (1951), Strommen, et. al. (1972), Greeley, McCready and McCourt (1976), Stark (1971), and Glock and Stark (1966).

In the process of trying to formulate a question you may also want to read a provocative essay by Watson (1931). In this old essay, the writing is in some places arrogant and in some places quaint, but in 20 pages, he raises perhaps a hundred questions for research that are still interesting.

CHAPTER IV

HAS ANYONE THOUGHT OF IT BEFORE?
REVIEWING THE LITERATURE

Introduction

Once you know what the question is, you should find out if anyone has ever researched a similar or related question, and what they found out. You should also find out what is known about the key concepts that are part of your question. For example, if your thesis has something to do with small churches, read several recent studies about the small church. If your thesis has something to do with belief, read some recent psychological studies of belief. Even if the studies you read do not relate directly to your research question, you will find the conceptual background provided by other researchers helpful.

It is quite likely that someone has researched a question similar to yours, and by studying their efforts, you can refine your question and make it much more powerful.

First Steps

Identify the key concepts in your question, and find out what names are given to these concepts in the research literature. If your thesis is related to the fields of psychology, sociology or education, you might find that your question sounds quite different when translated into the jargon of the field. For example, if you want to know what psychologists think about "pride" or "high self esteem," your reading should include articles on "internal locus of control." Perhaps the most efficient way to find out about alternative names for your key concepts is by talking with a scholar in the field. You can also skim an introductory textbook in the field.

Once you have your list of key concepts, use the literature search tools most readily available. Start with the card catalog in your seminary library. Also, see what's in your local public library. If you are near a college or university, take an initial look at their card catalog. Don't forget to look through a list of the D. Min. theses that have already been done at your seminary. And ask for bibliographic suggestions from your professors and fellow students.

You will probably end up with a fairly high stack of material to skim. In addition to noting the conclusions the authors reached and the basis for these conclusions, pay particular attention to their bibliographies. They may cite a source that will strongly influence the direction of your study. Also, if they include copies of questionnaires they have used, study them for suggestions in designing your own questionnaire.

Taming the Bibliography

Preparing a bibliography is usually drudgery. It is the last thing you do before the paper is finished, and it's hard to convince yourself that it's not a waste of time. Inevitably you find that you forgot to note a date, publisher, or page number, and under the pressure of a deadline, have to hunt for the missing information. Then, when you think you are finished, you find that you have left out one item.

Here is the best way I have found to handle the "bibliography blues."

Maintain your bibliographic file on 5" x 7" file cards. Every time you identify a potential bibliographic citation, type it at the top of the plain side of the card, using the style prescribed by your style manual. Do not write anything else on this side of the card.

On the back, write the name of the library or other location where you found it, and what the library call number is. This information will save you much time if you need to look it up again. Use the rest of the back side for appropriate notes.

Whenever you submit a draft of a chapter, or the entire thesis, for comments, prepare the bibliography by "fanning out" the necessary bibliographic cards and photocopying them. The only time you will have to

50

re-type the bibliography is when you type the final copy of the thesis.

This system is almost as efficient as buying a word processor, and much less expensive.

Some Useful Literature Search Tools

Dissertation Abstracts International

Dissertation Abstracts International (DAI) includes abstracts of all doctoral dissertations written at most graduate schools in the United States and Canada. The abstracts are written by the authors of the dissertations, and in some cases they contain sufficient information to make the abstract itself worthy of citation in your bibliography. In any case, the abstract will tell you whether or not it would be helpful for you to read the dissertation.

Each monthly issue of DAI includes an index, and the Comprehensive Dissertation Index (CDI) is a multi-volume index to all dissertations in DAI. Both DAI and CDI include an author index. In addition, they index dissertations by key words in the title. For example, index reference to the words "calling," "evaluation," "expectations," "pastoral," "performance," and "study" would lead you to the abstract numbered DA8219996, on page 1192-A, of the October, 1982, issue of DAI (Figure 4-1).

Of all the words in the title, you would probably only think of looking up "pastoral," and then only if you were interested in "pastoral counseling," "pastoral epistles," "pastoral calling," or some other topic for which "pastoral" is part of the standard description. But if your topic is concerned with pastoral calling, you would be able to find Shirkey's abstract. If the abstract suggests that you should read the full dissertation, you can purchase a microfilm or hard copy through University Microfilms (ordering instructions are in each issue of DAI), you can see if it is available through inter-library loan, or you can visit the library of the university that granted the degree.

51

A STUDY AND EVALUATION OF EXPECTATIONS AND
PERFORMANCE IN PASTORAL CALLING
Order No. DA821999
SHIRKEY, RONALD EUGENE, D.MIN. Drew University, 1982. 167pp.

This project was designed and conducted to provide a theoretical
and practical base for changing expectations, both those held
personally and those perceived to be held by others, and/or
performance in the aspect of ministry commonly known as pastoral
calling. During twenty-five years of ministry the writer had
experienced a gap between what was expected and what was done in
this area. Particular attention was given, in the project, to the place o
pastoral initiative; and, also, to what extent the problem may simply b
methodological.

Extensive research of available literature resulted in the setting
aside of the traditional 'shepherding' image of pastoral care, in favor
of the development of the concept of 'Affirmation' as an adequate
biblical/theological foundation for pastoral calling. This was then
examined in its historical, sociological, and psychological
perspectives.

A Project Committee--eight members of Christ Lutheran Church,
Monroe, Michigan--was utilized to provide guidance and support
throughout the project. This group, another congregational group,
and two clergy groups provided data concerning perceptions and
expectations in pastoral calling. In addition, calls were made by the
pastor on thirty families of the congregation, and evaluations were
made by him of those calls.

Project and leadership evaluation was provided by: each of the
four groups, as concerned the group meetings; the Project
Committee, as concerned the total project; and the pastor.

As a result of the project, Initiative was redefined and came to be
seen as a component of all pastoral calls. The project demonstrated
that the pastor who is freed from a sense of compulsion, real or
imaginary; released from the burden of faulty expectations; and
equipped with adequate time management tools; will find that three
things will happen, in terms of pastoral calling: more calls will be
made, more caring and helping will result from those calls, and there
will be a greater sense of celebration over the ministry that occurs.

Figure 4-1. Sample abstract from Dissertation
Abstracts International. Note. The
dissertation title and abstract
contained here is published with permission of University Microfilms
International, publishers of Dissertation Abstracts International (copyright ©1982 by University Microfilms
International), and may not be reproduced without their prior permission.

DAI is published in two sections. Section "A" includes dissertation abstracts from fields that we might call the "humanities." Section "B" covers the "sciences." Most of your references will probably be in section "A," but don't ignore section "B." Psychology is part of section "B," and it is quite possible that you will find a useful citation there. For example, if you are concerned about how people in your congregation understand salvation, you may want to compare their views with views in the dissertation by Margaret St. John (1982). See Figure 4-2.

BEING SAVED: ACCOUNTS OF RELIGIOUS EXPERIENCE IN AN APPALACHIAN VALLEY Order No. DA8215092

ST. JOHN, MARGARET SEYMOUR, PH.D. *The University of Michigan,* 1982. 161pp. Co-Chairpersons: Raphael S. Ezekiel, Lois W. Hoffman

Accounts of the religious experience of being saved were collected over a three-year period of fieldwork in a rural, coal-mining Missionary Baptist community in East Tennessee. Several accounts are presented and discussed from two vantage points. First the experience itself is sequentially divided into phases and then examined as a whole for its social, developmental and personal meanings within the history of the valley. Then the accounts and narrators are reviewed for differences among them. Four groups are distinguished on the basis of degree of hypnotic susceptibility, verbal giftedness and empathy. One very rich account details a theme of developmental transition. The richest and most spiritual account is finally presented for its example as a therapeutic encounter and its contribution to a psychodynamic model of therapy.

Figure 4-2. Sample abstract of dissertation dealing with psychology of religion. (Reprinted with permission of University Microfilms International).

You should pay particular attention to section "B" if your interest is in pastoral counseling. For example, Wang's 1983 study of qualities related to effectiveness in pastoral counseling was abstracted on page 2011-B of the December, 1982 issue of DAI (see Figure 4-3).

DEMOGRAPHIC, PERCEPTUAL, AND RELIGIOUS
DETERMINANTS OF PASTORAL COUNSELING
Order No. DA8225523
WANG, PO HONG, PH.D. *Fuller Theological Seminary, School of Psychology*, 1983. 119pp.

This study extended Malony's (1964) investigation of the relationship among beliefs, attitudes, and pastoral counseling. Two actresses, portraying the role of a parishioner, were counseled by twenty-one pastors enrolled in a Doctor of Ministry program. The pastors were asked to respond to the actresses as if they were parishioners seeking pastoral counseling. Each pastor was video-taped for three successive one-half hour interviews. The videotapes were rated on Accurate Empathy, Non-Possessive Warmth, and Self-Congruence (Truax and Carkhuff, 1967) by three qualified judges.

The ratings were related to (a) demographic variables: years in ministerial service, pastoral counseling training, and graduate counseling training; (b) perceptual variables: pastoral counseling role perception, positive view of human nature, personal ratings of effectiveness in pastoral counseling, and overall pastoral job satisfaction; (c) religious variables: tendency to view God gracious and available, tendency to believe human beings as potentially good and needing enlightenment, amount of energy devoted to religious considerations, emphasis on the divine in one's religious life, and the appropriate use of religious resources.

There were some sample characteristics (such as sample size and homogeneity) which possibly confounded these results. However, if they be taken as valid several comments could be made. This study is noteworthy for what it did not find as well as for what it did.

First, demographic variables, such as experience and training, are not adequate predictors of counseling effectiveness among pastors.

Second, the lone perceptual dimension, namely having a negative outlook towards others, while perhaps more realistic, was found related to being open, honest, and authentic but not necessarily to being empathetic and warm.

Third, the appropriate use of religious resources is negatively related to effective pastoral counseling. The results suggest a serious lack of integration between practical theology and counseling practice.

Figure 4-3.   Sample abstract of dissertation
dealing with pastoral counseling.
(Reprinted with permission of
University Microfilms International).

Psychological Abstracts

Psychological Abstracts indexes and provides abstracts of a wide variety of literature. The entire contents of some journals are abstracted. In addition, a large number of journals are reviewed, and selected articles are abstracted. Some doctoral dissertations are indexed, and abstracts are provided for material that was published in languages other than English.

Publications are indexed by topic, and under each topic, all of the concepts with which a publication deals are listed, followed by the abstract number. Figure 4-4 is a portion of a sample page from a Psychological Abstracts subject index, the index for July through December, 1982, p. 742. The subjects on this page include "religion," "religiosity," "religious affiliation," "religious beliefs," "religious education," and "religious literature." If you examine this page, you will get a good idea of the type of material you might expect to find by using Psychological Abstracts.

Reliability (Test) [See Test Reliability]
Religion [See Also Related Terms]
amount of alcohol consumed & frequency & consequences of drinking & help sought & age of vignette individual & Ss' own drinking habits & religion, perception of seriousness of drinking, college students, 12594
anthropomorphism vs concept of supernatural realm as defining features in religion, cognitive theory of religion, comment on article by S. Guthrie, 12487
benefits of employer compliance with employee religious accommodation requests, 13818
construc ive & neurotic aspects of religion, psychoanalytic theory & practi e & views of K. Horney, 1660
definitic 1 of religion as anthropomorphism, cognitive theory of religi 'n, reply to criticism by R. H. Crapo, 12489
Image Dei as foundation to psychotherapy, 4025
influer ce of Freud's hermeneutic of suspicion on writings of theologian J. Segundo, 12500
interface of psychiatry & religion, development of new psychiatry residency training program, 13569
perceived value of religious vs informational solutions to hypothetical female's personal problem, college students, 12634
phenomenological analysis, religious experiencing, 3463
philosophical assumptions & religious beliefs of Bi/Polar personality theory, 12672

55

psychological factors, failure of expected miracle to occur, 12488
psychology of religion, review of recent books, Netherlands, 8015
public opinion about religion, US, 1974–81, 3454
religion in introductory psychology texts, 1950's vs 1970's, 2080
religious implications of K. Horney's theory, comment on B G.
  Wood's paper, 1646
role of religion, coping with bereavement after death of spouse, 8017
trends in labor force participation & family organization & religious
  participation & interest in Africa, Black females, 1059
Religiosity
coping behavior & adequacy of social networks & income & religious
  commitment, adjustment to bereavement in death of spouse,
  elderly, literature review, 7938
early familial disruption & religiosity of male & sexual prejudices &
  ignorance & communication problems, rigid sexual behavior,
  sexually dysfunctional vs functional 19–64 yr old couples, 1482
ethical & diagnostic problems, treatment, ultrareligious socially
  maladjusted 19 yr old males referred unwillingly for psychiatric
  treatment, Israel, 1635
fraternity/sorority membership & sex & religiosity & place of
  residence & day-time vs night-time enrollment & socioeconomic
  status, attitudes toward premarital sex, college students, 3502
issues in analysis of identity transformation in authoritarian religious
  groups when viewed as brainwashing cults, 3467
neurotic aspects of religiosity & conversion as seen in noncyclic
  uterine bleeding, 26 yr old Jewish female whose parents were
  concentration camp inmates, 1525
public opinion about religion, US, 1974–81, 3454

Figure 4-4. Sample Portion of a page from a semi-
annual index to Psychological
Abstracts. Note. This citation is
reprinted with permission of the
American Psychological Association,
publisher of Psychological Abstracts
and the PsycINFO Database (Copyright
© by the American Psychological
Association), and may not be reproduced without its prior permission.

    In using Psychological Abstracts, your first task
is to decide what topics to examine. Among the topics
of potential general interest to D. Min. researchers
that have been indexed in Psychological Abstracts are
those listed in Table 4-1. In addition, try subjects
that relate especially to your research topic, such as
"aging" or "groups."

Table 4-1

Selected Index Terms Used in Psychological Abstracts

(RELIGION)	(ETHICS/MORALITY/VALUES)
Hinduism	Allport-Vernon-Lindzey
Prayer	Altruism
Zen Buddhism	Asceticism
Buddhism	Charitable Behavior
Bible	Conscience
Religious Literatrue	Human Potential Movement
Christianity	Deception
Judaism	Dishonesty
Roman Catholicism	Ethics
Clergy	Personal Values
Chaplains	Social Values
Lay Religious Personnel	Values
Ministers	Morality
Priests	Gambling
Religiosity	Hedonism
Religious Practices	Moral Development
Rabbis	Pacifism
Nuns	
Evangelists	
Missionaries	
Yoga	

(THEOLOGY/PHILOSOPHY)	(COUNSELING)
Existentialism	Consciousness Raising Groups
Religious Beliefs	Pastoral Counseling
Witchcraft	Premarital Counseling
Glossolalia	Counselor Attitudes
God Concepts	Counselor Characteristics
Humanism	Crisis Intervention
Metaphysics	Suicide Prevention
Occultism	Death and Dying
Philosophies	Death Anxiety
Pragmatism	Death Attitudes
Meditation	Death Education
Reductionism	Help Seeking Behavior
Superstitions	Transactional Analysis
Fundamentalism	Privileged Communication
Atheism	Marriage Counseling
Liberalism	Logotherapy
	Irrational Beliefs
	Counseling Psychology

57

Counselor Education
Clinical Methods Training
Community Mental Health
Conjoint Therapy

(FAMILY)   (COMMUNICATION)

Premarital Counseling   Drama
Marital Counseling   Leadership Style
Extramarital Intercourse   Opinion/Attitude/Interest Survey
Promiscuity   Persuasive Communication
Marital Conflict   Aesthetics
Marriage Rites   Public Relations
Parent-Child Relations   Arts
Parental Role   Audiences
Role Models   Humor
                                  Censorship
                                  Symbolism

(EDUCATION/TEACHING)   (OTHER)

Educational Psychology   Emotional Content
Personality Development   Faith Healing
Human Relations Training   Geriatrics
Lesson Plans   Gerontology
Seminaries   Magical Thinking
                                  Self Actualization
                                  Aged
                                  Older People
                                  Tolerance for Ambiguity
                                  Authoritarianism
                                  Dogmatism
                                  Openmindedness

Note. Source: Thesaurus of Psychological Index Terms (3rd ed.).
Washington, D.C.: American Psychological Association, 1982.

Select half a dozen of the most promising
subjects, and pursue them through the cumulative
indexes and the indexes to individual volumes. Note
the numbers of potentially useful abstracts. Figure
4-5 is a fairly typical abstract, indexed under the
heading of "religion" in Figure 4-4. It is found on
page 884 of the October, 1982, issue, and might be an
important reference for a pastoral counseling D. Min.
project.

8017. **Van Uden, M. H. & Spitters, P. J.** (Katholieke U Nijmegen Psychologisch Lab, Vakgroep Cultuur- en Godsdienstpsychologie, Netherlands) **De rol van het religieuze zingevingssysteem in crisisverwerking. Een exploratief onderzoek door middel van deipte-interviews. / The role of the religious meaning system in coping with crisis: An exploratory study by means of depth interviews.** (Duth) *Gedrag: Tijdschrift voor Psychologie,* 1982, Vol 10(1–2), 17–38. —Discusses the role of religion in coping with bereavement after the death of a spouse. This is illustrated by 2 case studies. In the first, findings indicate a h;althy grief process, in the second a pathological process. Relig on is placed within a broader frame of reference by defining it ;s a complex of meaning systems. The relation between tradition.;l religion and religion as a complex of meaning systems is discu'sed, using concepts from the theory of Symbolic Interactionism. It is concluded that if one wants to understand the function of religion in grief, one must look at the place of religion in the total personality. Humanity chooses from religious tradition that which fits best. This may be used for coping with grief. (16 ref) —*Journal abstract.*

Figure 4-5.   Sample of an abstract published
in Psychological Abstracts.
Note. This citation is reprinted
with permission of the American Psychological Association, publisher of
Psychological Abstracts and the Psyc-
INFO Database (Copyright © by the
American Psychological Association),
and may not be reproduced without
its prior permission.

Although most abstracts are for English language articles, a large number of abstracts are for articles written in other languages. This is true of #8017, in Figure 4-5. If such an article appears to be particularly important, and you cannot find the journal in any local library, try to get it through inter-library loan. Once you have the article, if you do not know the language, you can hire a translator through a local university or international center.

The abstracts should give you enough information so you can decide which publications you want to obtain and read in full.

Sociological Abstracts

Sociological Abstracts, published five times a year, indexes articles from sociological journals as well as selected articles from journals in related social scientific fields and the humanities. The contents are organized into 31 major categories, including "sociology of religion."

If you are "browsing," the "sociology of religion" section would be a good place to start. However, if your thesis topic is fairly will focused, each issue has a subject index which refers you to the article's code number. To find the code number location, refer to the table of contents.

Figure 4-6 shows three typical abstracts, all from the "sociology of religion" section of the December, 1982, issue of Sociological Abstracts (Volume 30, number 5).

Sociological Abstracts will be particularly useful if you are concerned about a social issue or phenomenon as it relates to your church. Such phenomena might include abortion, aging, death, equality, family, farms, feminism, homosexuality, human rights, humor, marriage, peace, poverty, prison, racism, or television, all of which were included in the December, 1982, index. The Sociological Abstracts index is not comprehensive, and you should definitely examine the table of contents and read the titles in the sections that promise to be most fruitful.

Resources in Education (ERIC)

ERIC (Educational Resources Information Center) is a U.S. Government supported organization that collects documents of interest to the field of education, abstracts and indexes them, and makes them available on microfiche and in hard copy. For the most part, these documents are unpublished manuscripts, such as papers presented at conventions. Some books and other published materials are also included.

Resources in Education is the monthly publication

82M6342

Cantrell, Randolph, Krile, James & Donohue, George (U Minnesota, Minneapolis 55455). The Community Involvement of Yoked Parishes, *Rural Sociology*, 1982, 47, 1, spring, 81-90.

¶ Sharing pastoral services is a common organizational response of churches facing declining resources & rising costs. This research describes the negative effects yoked parish arrangements have on civic involvement, ecumenical programs, giving, & issue involvement among 131 Ru Minn congregations. The limitations placed on the pastoral role by multiple-point service are discussed, especially as regards the pastor's boundary-spanning administrative functions. Pastoral presence is shown to be associated with the level of civic activity in yoked parishes. 5 Tables. HA

82M6387

Newman, William M. & Wright, Stuart A. (U Connecticut, Storrs 06268). The Effects of Sermons among Lay Catholics: An Exploratory Study, *Review of Religious Research*, 1980, 22, 1, Sept, 54-59.

¶ The effects of sermons on a 1976 sample of lay Catholics is examined using questionnaire data (N = 1,575) It was found that sermons have rather a moderate effect & that social variables such as educational attainment, marital status, & involvement in parish activities are useful predictors of sermon effectiveness Although the findings are based on a purposive rather than random sample, they raise some important considerations for both future research on sermon effectiveness & policymaking. 3 Tables. Modified HA

82M6389

Perry, Everett L. & Hoge, Dean R., Faith Priorities of Pastor and Laity as a Factor in the Growth or Decline of Presbyterian Congregations, *Review of Religious Research*, 1981, 22, 3, Mar, 221-232.

¶ Questionnaire data from 204 Presbyterian congregations were used to assess the importance of various aspects of faith & theology for congregational growth or decline over a 6-year period. Data included self-reports by pastors & laity plus ratings of each by the other. None of the faith priorities & theological views strongly correlated with congregational growth. The few weak associations that occurred were consistent with Dean Kelley's theories that conservative theology & avoidance of social action are conducive to growth (*Why Conservative Churches Are Growing*, 2nd edition, New York: Harper & Row, 1977). Measures of pastor-lay differences were unimportant except for differences between laity's ratings of their self-reports on the question of social action. HA

Figure 4-6. Three sample abstracts from Sociological Abstracts. Note. Reprinted by permission of Sociological Abstracts.

61

of the abstracts. Each issue has a subject index, and annual subject indexes are also available.

Although this service may sound too specialized to be of use to the typical D. Min. student, it includes a broad variety of material. For example, consider the three abstracts illustrated in Figure 4-7, all published in 1981. They deal with pastoral counseling (ED 195 882), growth in the ministerial profession (ED 204 509), and religion and mental health (ED 205 446).

One of the most important pieces of information in these abstracts is the "ED" number at the upper left. Some academic libraries maintain microfiche files of all ERIC documents, and they will be filed in numerical order. If you need to order a copy from ERIC, the "ED" number is your order number. Because of this, the "ED" number should be listed in the bibliographic citation.

The "descriptor" lists with the three abstracts in Figure 4-7 will give you some sense of the range of subjects indexed in ERIC.

ED 195 882   CG 014 834
Pierce, Norma F.
Preference for Pastoral Counseling Roles as Perceived by Male and Female Adults.
Pub Date—Mar 80
Note—11p.; Paper presented at the Annual Meeting of the Southeastern Psychological Association (26th, Washington, DC, March 26-29, 1980).
Pub Type— Reports - Research (143) — Speeches/-Meeting Papers (150)
EDRS Price - MF01/PC01 Plus Postage.
Descriptors—Adults, *Attitude Measures, *Church Role, *Clergy, *Counseling Services, *Family Relationship, Questionnaires, *Sex Differences. Social Services, Spouses
Forty-six adults responded to a questionnaire in which they ranked their preferred counseling person in four problem areas: home or work, children, spiritual matters, and marital problems. Males' first choice in all areas was their spouse; females chose their spouse for work and child problems, their pastor for spiritual matters, and themselves for marital problems. Results from the opinionnaire indicate a desire for trained counselors in local churches. A female counselor was preferred by 59% of the females and 34% of the males. In most churches, counseling services were offered only by pastors. There appears to be a need not only for trained counselors in churches but for women in this role. (Author/CS)

Figure 4-7. Sample abstracts from ERIC.

ED 204 509   CE 029 383
Malcomson, William L.
Growing in Ministry. Reflections Based on Current
  Research.
Center for the Ministry (American Baptist Chur-
  ches), Oakland, Calif.
Pub Date—[81]
Note—20p.
Pub Type— Opinion Papers (120)
EDRS Price - MF01/PC01 Plus Postage.
Descriptors—*Clergy, Competence, Feedback, *In-
  dividual Development, Peer Influence, *Profes-
  sional Continuing Education, *Professional
  Development, *Theological Education
  Growing in ministry is wholistic, as ministry is
wholistic. Ministry is a calling and profession, and
continuing education in ministry must be of help in
both areas. Both attitudinal and behavioral growing
should be considered–attitudinal as it has to do with
a minister's being, calling, person, sense of worth,
and spirituality; and behavioral as it has to do with
a minister's doing, profession, job, skill employ-
ment, and competence. Contemporary research
shows too much emphasis on professionalism and
neglect of the spiritual formation of ministers.
Growing in ministry should be self-directed. There
is also a need for collegiality in the growing-learning
process. Such feedback, concern, and correction
from other professionals and lay persons are necessary for growth. Finally, ministers should realize
that there are obstacles to growth and crises to
which they are subject, but that the pain caused by
these obstacles and crises is a necessary part of
growing. (YLB)

ED 205 446   SO 013 522
Summerlin, Florence A., Comp
Religion and Mental Health: A Bibliography.
National Inst. on Alcohol Abuse and Alcoholism
  (DHEW/PHS), Rockville, Md.; National Inst. on
  Drug Abuse (DHEW/PHS), Rockville, Md.
Pub Date—80
Note—402p.
Available from—Superintendent of Documents,
  U.S. Government Printing Office, Washington,
  DC 20402 ($8.50).
Pub Type— Reference Materials - Bibliographies
  (131)
EDRS Price - MF01/PC17 Plus Postage.
Descriptors—Annotated Bibliographies, Attitudes,
  Clergy, Death, Drug Abuse, Marriage, *Mental
  Health, Older Adults, *Religion, Religious Edu-
  cation, Religious Factors, Suicide

Figure 4-7. (continued)

63

This annotated bibliography cites journal articles, reports, and books on religion and mental health published since 1970. The listing is intended to help psychologists, psychiatrists, clergymen, social workers, teachers, doctors and other professionals respond to requests for information and advice in areas spanning the common ground between religion and mental health. The bibliography is organized by topical areas. These include: attitudes toward religion; the clergy (their careers, education and training. and personalities); death. suicide and bereavement; drug and alcohol use; eastern religious traditions; elderly; ethical and legal issues; interdisciplinary collaboration; marriage and family counseling; mental health ministry; theoretical, theological and psychological issues of religion; mental health; religious education; religious experiences (altered states of consciousness, conversion and Pentecostal events); religious practices and rituals; sects and cults; sexology; and social issues. A listing of nonprint resources is provided. The bibliography concludes with subject and author indexes. (Author/RM).

Figure 4-7. (continued)

Religious and Theological Abstracts

Published four times a year, Religious and Theological Abstracts provides abstracts primarily from theological journals, although it also abstracts articles in journals of empirical research, such as Review of Religious Research and Journal for the Scientific Study of Religion. Each issue is divided into four sections: "Biblical," "Theological," "Historical," and "Practical." The "Practical" section is further divided into (a) "The Ministry," (b) "Homiletics," (c)"Worship," (with four subdivisions), (d) "Pastoral Care" (with two subdivisions), (e) "Church Administration," (f) "Education" (with four subdivisions), (g) "Mission" (with four subdivisions), and (h) "Religion and Culture" (with nine subdivisions). "Religion and Culture" is cross referenced to "Ethics" in the "Theological" section. The fourth issue each year includes a subject index, an author index and a scripture index. There is no indication as to which (if any) journals are fully abstracted and which are abstracted selectively.

Figure 4-8 is a typical abstract (from Volume 25,

number 4, Winter 1982). "RQ" following the article's title indicates the article was published in Restoration Quarterly.

3624 Moore, Michael S. (Whitehall, PA) BASIC ATTITUDES TO-WARD "FOREIGNERS" AMONG SELECTED CHURCHES OF CHRIST. RQ, 1981, 24(4):225-238. A mono cultural outlook hinders a local church-family's efforts to evangelize effectively among local ethnic units. But, a linguistic tool (i.e. a carefully designed questionnaire) can help local pastors and their flocks to evaluate their relative level of appreciation for local ethnic units. And, when such an awareness is awakened local church leaders can more easily recognize the need for proper training in preparation for their tasks. The tool was tested among 19 Churches of Christ—10 in a control group and 9 in the Mid-South group. The control group was significantly more multi cultural in its attitudes toward "foreigners" than were the respondent Christians in the Mid-South. SLL

Figure 4-8. Sample abstract from Religious and Theological Abstracts. Note. Reprinted by permission of Religious and Theological Abstracts, Inc., Myerstown, PA 17067, J.C. Christman, Editor.

Science of Religion: Abstracts and Index of Recent Articles

This is a highly selective international abstract published in Amsterdam under the auspices of the International Association for the History of Religions. Very few articles abstracted will be relevant to D. Min. projects, but since each issue has a good topical index, and since it abstracts international journals not abstracted elsewhere, it deserves some consideration in your literature review.

Handbook of Research on Religious Development

This handbook (Strommen, 1971) consists of 22 articles on the then current status of research on various topics bearing some relation to religious education. Articles average 40 pages, including extensive bibliographies of published research.

65

Article titles include "Psychological Interpretations of Religious Experience," "Delayed Gratification: A Psychological and Religious Analysis," "The Religious Effects of Parochial Education," "Religion, Prejudice and Personality," "Religion and Psychological Health," and "Religious Practices."

This volume is a valuable tool in the literature review for a thesis that deals with the individual characteristics of church members, rather than dealing with groups or with the church as an institution.

Master's Theses in Education

An index published annually since 1951-52 by Research Publications, Cedar Falls, Iowa. Originally under the auspices of the Bureau of Research, Iowa State Teachers College, but the school is no longer listed in the title page. Herbert M. Silvey has been an editor since the first issue, so the format has been consistent from the beginning.

"Education" is a much broader field than one might realize, and this index contains rich resources for the D. Min. researcher. You might be particularly interested in theses indexed under "adult education," "religious education," "delinquency," "family life and sex education," and "moral and ethical values." The following titles might suggest the breadth of topics included in the thesis:

> Angel, Steven P., The Relation of Childhood Church Attendance and Adult Church Attendance, Muncie, IN: Ball State University (1979-80).

> Ball, Laurie H., A Course Designed to Aid Morally Conservative Parents in Their Role as Sex Educators, Provo, UT: Brigham Young University (1980-81).

> Fasth, Mary C., The Effect of a Personal and Spiritual Growth Training Program for Parish Lay Ministers on Variables Measured by the Personal Orientation Inventory, Chicago: De Paul University (1981-82).

Taylor, Roger H., Study of the Effectiveness
of a Project to Encourage Clergymen to
Minister to Developmentally Disabled
Persons, Milwaukee: Cardinal Stritch
College (1979-80).

Annual Review of Research in Religious Education

You may find this a useful source even if your
field is not religious education. It consists of
abstracts of published empirical research which is
relevant to the religious education field. Most of
the research was published in secular journals. This
abstracting project was conceived as a way to update
Strommen (1971), so it includes abstracts of research
published after 1969.

Two volumes have been published (Peatling, 1980,
1981). Additional volumes have been prepared, but a
lack of funds has kept them from reaching print.
Between them, the two volumes contain 216 abstracts,
in addition to bibliographic references to research
for which abstracts are not available. At this point,
there is no subject index.

Psychological Studies of Clergymen

Menges and Dittes (1965) is a highly useful
reference to older research. It includes
approximately 700 abstracts of research on clergy.
Seventy five percent of the abstracted studies were
published between 1955 and 1965. The research studies
were classified into several categories, including
unique characteristics of clergy, effectiveness of
clergy, differences among clergy, problems of clergy
(Menges and Dittes label this category
"consequences"), counseling and therapy, mental health
and illness, and wives and family.

The scope of this volume of abstracts probably
covers 50% of the most popular D. Min. research
subjects.

Coville, et. al. (1968, pp. 137-164) added 312
references to Catholic studies, updating the biblio-

graphy to February, 1967. Their 527 item bibliography includes only Catholic studies, and is not annotated or divided topically.

Abstracts of Research in Pastoral Care and Counseling

Volume I of this annual publication was issued in 1972. A topical index has been published to cover the first ten volumes. The abstracts are arranged by topic, and include the researcher's address, so you can inquire for further information.

This abstract series is published by the Joint Council on Research in Pastoral Care and Counseling. For more information, write them at P.O. Box 5184 (507 North Lombardy Street), Richmond, Virginia 23220.

Religion and Society in North America

I have not seen this. I have only seen a brief review in The Christian Century (July 6-13, 1983, p.660), and it seems worth mentioning here. The editor is Robert de V. Brunkow. It is a reference book that abstracts 4,304 articles on American religion from 1973 through 1980. The review says that it is well indexed. I assume seminary libraries will be adding it to their collections.

Periodicals

In addition to searching abstracts, indexes, and other bibliographic sources, some periodicals merit an issue-by-issue review. These journals frequently publish material related to potential D. Min. projects, so that it is worth some time to skim their tables of contents, in case there is a crucial article you missed in the abstracts and indexes.

Journal for the Scientific Study of Religion (JSSR). Published quarterly since 1961 by the Society for the Scientific Study of Religion. It has been heavily sociological, although psychological research has been reported with increasing frequency in recent years. A 20-year index, 1961-1981, has been published.

Review of Religious Research (RRR). Published quarterly since 1959 by the Religious Research Association. A 20-year index was published in 1979. There has been a tendency for RRR to focus on institutional issues within the church, and for JSSR to focus on the broader relations among religion, the individual, and society. This distinction is no longer as sharp as it once was.

Sociological Analysis, subtitled "A Journal in the Sociology of Religion," published since 1940 by the Association for the Sociology of Religion. Prior to 1971, the name of the sponsoring association was "The American Catholic Sociological Society." It now publishes both Catholic and Protestant research. An index was published in 1981.

Social Compass, subtitled "International Review of Sociology of Religion," published since 1953 by the Centre de Recherches Socio-Religieuses, Unversite Catholique de Louvain, Belgium. Articles in English and French. In general, the articles are less directly relevant to typical D. Min. projects than those of other journals mentioned here, but the journal is worth surveying. For example, if you are looking for an approach to the study of sermon content, read "The Content of the Parochial Sermons in the Evangelical Lutheran Church of Finland as Indicators of the Openness and Closeness [sic] of the Church as System" (1980, 27, pp. 417-435). If by some chance, your project deals with hymnology, read "Religious and Social Attitudes in 'Hymns Ancient and Modern' (1889)" (1975, 22, pp. 211-236). Each issue includes an extensive international bibliography of articles on the sociology of religion, arranged by subject. A 20-year index to Social Compass was published in 1973.

Journal of Psychology and Theology, published quarterly since 1973, by the Rosemead Graduate School of Psychology. Each issue includes both theoretical and research articles. A 1973-1982 index was included in the Winter, 1982 issue (10, pp. 387-427). It indicates that 51 research articles were published in that time. This limited number means the journal is probably a less fruitful source than JSSR and RRR, but it is worth examining.

Leadership, published quarterly since 1980 by
Christianity Today, Inc., is a practical journal for
pastors that includes some data-based articles.
Almost all of the articles can suggest D. Min.
projects.

PRRC Emerging Trends, published monthly since
January, 1979, by the Princeton Religious Research
Center. It is a four to six page newsletter
presenting data related to religious life obtained by
Gallup International. Such survey data are sometimes
superficial, particularly when reporting on subjects
as complex as religious belief. For example, the
question, "How important would you say religion is in
your own life? -- very important, fairly important, or
not very important," leaves one wondering in what
different senses various people consider religion to
be important or not important. (See the section in
Chapter 6, "How Religious are People?"). However, when
response to the same question over a period of 30
years is presented (1983, 5 (1), p.5) and can be
compared with other data (such as church membership)
over the same period, it at least provides a basis for
further questions. Emerging Trends is clearly laid
out and easy to survey.

How to Obtain Publications

If you live in an urban area that includes more
than one institution of higher education, most of the
journals will be available either in bound volumes or
microform. Ask your librarian if there is a listing
that tells which journals are located at various
institutions in your area. Journal articles may also
be available through interlibrary loan.

Articles from more than 10,000 journals can be
ordered from University Microfilms International. A
number of the journals of greatest potential interest
to D. Min. researchers are not on their list, but the
list is being expanded continuously. For information
on their article and issue reprint service, write to
300 North Zeeb Road, Ann Arbor, Michigan 48106.

Many of the articles indexed in Sociological
Abstracts can be obtained from the abstract service.
For information, see any issue of Sociological Abstracts.

Dissertations and theses can sometimes be obtained through interlibrary loan. Most doctoral dissertations and some master's theses can be purchased as either microfilm or hard copy from University Microfilms International. Microfilm and microfiche are much less expensive than hard copy, so if you must purchase, consider microform seriously. Microfilm and microfiche readers may be available at your public library, seminary, college, or even some businesses.

CHAPTER V

WHAT DOCTRINAL ASSUMPTIONS HAVE I MADE?
THE RELATION BETWEEN THEOLOGY AND
EMPIRICAL RESEARCH

The Function of Theology

The doctrinal basis of the D. Min. thesis will do one or two things. It will either establish a frame of reference, or it will pose an empirical question, or both.

Frame of Reference

The frame of reference is primary, even though it is sometimes appropriate to leave it unstated. The frame of reference is a way of viewing an empirical situation. This way of viewing the situation is arbitrary in the sense that others can employ a different frame of reference and make sense of the world on a temporary basis, at least. (This is not the place for an extended discussion of nominalism or phenomenology.) The alternative frames of reference may not be moral, or may not be healthy, or may be impractical in the long run. If so, it is appropriate to point these things out when you write your doctrinal chapter. It is more important that your stated frame of reference truly be the frame of reference from which your research develops.

The concept of the frame of reference was nicely illustrated by Katona (1944). He told of two U.S. merchants during World War II:

> Of two manufacturers of men's shirts, one, at the beginning of 1943, had lowered the quality of his product in order to save a few cents in the cost of each shirt. He had done this by buying cheaper fabrics, cutting down on workmanship, and eliminating collar linings. The other manufacturer had done nothing of the sort; in the Autumn of 1943, he was still making the same quality shirt as he had a year before.

73

Why had the first manufacturer changed the quality of his product? He explained his decision thus: "Every student of economics will readily understand that the function of a businessman is to make as much profit as possible. Likewise, there is no doubt about the fact that we have now what is called a seller's market; orders on hand are much larger than our current output, although we are working at full capacity. We could sell much more than we produce, but due to the war we cannot increase our output. Finally, there is price control: we are forbidden to raise our prices even though some of our expenses have increased and our customers would be willing to pay higher prices. I have been in business for 20 years; I always charged the highest price the market could bear; now for the first time I am forbidden to do so. Isn't it natural that I should save what I can on my expenses? Before the war competition made such savings impossible, but now in a seller's market, it's different."

In studying the businesss policy of the second manufacturer one might have expected to find certain differences in his market which would explain why he had acted differently. But this man described his business situation in the same way as his competitor. He could sell whatever he could produce at high prices, but, of course, he is subject to ceilings. True, some expenses increased; but, because of large volume and steady production, business is not unprofitable. "Price control is a good thing," said the second manufacturer. "It applies to the fabrics I buy as well as to the shirts I sell, and runaway prices would hurt my business. What I am most interested in is keeping the goodwill of my customers, which I am going to need very much when the war is over. That is why I scrupulously watch the quality of the fabrics I buy, and why the workmanship of my shirts will not deteriorate as long as I can help it."
(pp. 340-341.)

74

Developing the Frame of Reference

A D. Min. thesis certainly ought to have a theological basis. But in practice, many pastors even after the years of experience required as a prerequisite to entering the D. Min. program, are uncertain how to relate the theological basis to the question they are researching. Too often, the theological chapter seems to be simply "tacked on" to the rest of the thesis.

Helmut Thielicke expressed the basic problem well in a discussion of preaching:

> . . . what the preacher says in the pulpit must have a relationship to what fills the rest of his existence.... does he really live in his doctrinal house?... does he do his thinking, feeling, and willing in it? (1965, pp. 5-6.)

Similarly, we can ask whether the D. Min. thesis was written inside or outside of the doctrinal house.

How does the D. Min. researcher develop the theological basis for frame of reference? There are two approaches.

One is to develop the research question, then reflect on it and outline the theological basis. Then, in response, the question can be refined, the theological basis can be further developed, and the question can be further refined. This iterative process can be continued until the project is adequately defined. Such an exercise need not depend on the writings of an established theologian. The D. Min. student should have enough maturity to do an adequate job of theological analysis. Of course, it would be foolish to ignore insights to be gleaned from other theologians.

The biggest problem with this approach is the temptation to do post hoc theologizing. Ministers know how to use words well, and are generally able to write to meet a deadline. Since the D. Min. researcher feels secure with words, the temptation is to move immediately into the less certain arena of the project, complete the empirical study, and compose the theological justification the night before the written

75

report is due.

The second valid approach to developing a theological basis is to choose a theological guide, probably a published theologian with whom you agree. Take this person's writings as the doctrinal basis, and let these writings suggest the research question. Sometimes the research question will arise clearly from the theological writing. This is especially true when the theologian makes an assertion of fact that is worth investigating. A theological frame of reference may not suggest a clear question, but potential questions can be evaluated in light of the frame of reference.

The approach of this chapter is to briefly discuss several theological passages, suggesting how they might suggest a research project or an approach to a project. The writings were selected almost at random. The present author is not in sympathy with all of the theologians cited, although all represent serious work and are worthy of consideration. The criterion for selection was an informal attempt to present a variety of theological perspectives, in order to demonstrate that an appropriate D. Min. project can be developed around any theological position.

This is not to say that all theological topics will be equally fruitful. Writings on the doctrine of the church will provide more suggestions for projects in ministry than will writings about angels. But if you are really convinced that your theological guide has important things to say, then the things that guide says will have practical importance for your ministry, and will thus provide you with a number of appropriate D. Min. projects.

Working with a Frame of Reference

Dealing with a Normative Statement

Consider this passage:

. . . we are obliged in our preaching and in

76

our reflection to affirm the identity of
sola fide and sola gratia. Only thus can we
send out the call to believe without doing
injustice to the sovereignty of grace. For
divine salvation is preached in the urgent
appeal. Faith is fulfilled in this
salvation. Only in faith can we transcend
the entanglement which has so often dimmed
the light of divine salvation in the
history of the Church. (Berkouwer, 1954, p.
200.)

This is a "frame of reference" statement. The
passage is the conclusion of an extended discourse
about faith, grace, repentence, and justification in
Christian religion. In the discourse, Berkouwer's
sole concern is with humanity's relation to God. The
criteria for judging his arguments are those criteria
familiar to all seminary graduates: logical validity,
historical validity, scriptural validity.

Berkouwer's study is not explicitly concerned
with the work of the pastor, but certainly the above
passage has pastoral implications. The researcher who
accepts Berkouwer as a theological guide could
certainly use this as the frame of reference for a
parish research project. Among the questions
Berkouwer's discourse might raise are:

How are the concepts of "faith" and "grace"
understood in my parish?
How will these concepts be understood
following a carefully structured sermon
series?
How will these concepts be understood
following a carefully designed teaching
series?

The first question might be a preliminary one,
providing necessary information that will help you
gauge the effectiveness of your preaching or teaching.
If it is preliminary, you will strive for the simplest
possible way of answering it, consistent with
validity. You will probably administer a carefully
designed questionnaire.

The first question might also be seen as the
entire research project. In such a case, you would
use a variety of methods in the attempt to understand

people's functional concepts of "faith" and "grace."
You would certainly use a questionnaire, but you would
also probably interview people and do a content
analysis of the interviews. Since most people are not
accomplished at theological discourse, when you
analyze the interviews, you would look for personal
autobiographical statements that give a clue to how
they live with "faith" or "grace," even though they
may not use the words.

Of course, to do this, you yourself must have a
very clear understanding of the concepts, both as
understood by your theological guide (in this case,
Berkouwer), and as they might be understood by others.
Thus, theological analysis would be a necessary part
of your parish research project, rather than something
simply attached.

In your role as researcher, you would strive for
objectivity. For one thing, this means that in the
research interview, you must avoid the temptation to
teach the truth as presented by your theological
guide. The research interview is an attempt to learn
how the person being interviewed understands the
world. For another thing, you must try to dissociate
the responses of the person being interviewed with any
past disagreements you may have had with that person.
If you are that person's pastor, there may have been
disagreements between you and that person over matters
of church administration, policy, or other things. If
you have prejudged this person, the interview may be
worthless as a research tool.

Frame of Reference as a Basis for Evaluation

Suppose the D. Min. project is a program developed
within the church or among church members. One kind
of evaluative question is, "Is the church the
appropriate organization to do this program?" This is
a frame of reference question. To see how a thesis
might grow out of this question, consider how Richard
McBrien deals with the definition of the church.

The Church is the whole body, or congregation,
of persons who are called by God the Father to
acknowledge the Lordship of Jesus, the Son,
in word, in sacrament in witness, and in

78

service, and, through the power of the Holy
Spirit, to collaborate with Jesus' historic
mission for the sake of the Kingdom of God.
(McBrien, 1980, p. 714.)

Once McBrien develops his definition of the
church, he expounds some implications of that definition.
One implication is that the church ought to be
involved in social justice activities. What are the
appropriate boundaries of such activities? According
to McBrien:

... intervention in the social and political
orders must always be responsible, never
arbitrary, particularly in the light of the
Church's limited resources. Accordingly,
such intervention must be governed by the
following criteria: (1) The issue must be
clearly justice-related. (2) The
ecclesiastical agency or cluster of churches
should have the competence to deal with the
issue. (3) There should be sufficient
resources within the particular church(es)
to deal with the problem effectively. (4)
The issue should have a prior claim over
other justice-related problems which compete
for the Church's attention. (5) The form of
ecclesiastical action should not
unnecessarily or unduly polarize the Church
itself, since the church is always called to
be a sign of the Gospel and the Kingdom of
God. A diversity of viewpoints is to be
expected and tolerated, so that agreement
with the specific form of social of
political action selected by the church(es)
should not become itself a test of authentic
Christian faith and commitment. This is not
to say, on the other hand, that the mere
risk of conflict within the Church should
discourage such intervention. Conflict is
essential to growth. But excessive conflict
can be corrosive and finally destructive of
the unity of the Church itself. (1980, pp.
720,721.)

Such a frame of reference analysis provides a
basis for a useful program evaluation. If you were to
take McBrien as a theological guide, and if your
thesis project was to develop, evaluate, refine, and

79

report on a church based social action program, your report could be a careful analysis of the program in response to each of these five points.

The analysis can take many forms. The analysis of the first item will probably be philosophical. The second item, competence, may draw on analytical techniques established by academic disciplines as diverse as business administration, education, sociology, or political science, depending on the nature of the project. The fifth point, about polarization in the church, may call for a carefully designed questionnaire to be used with those involved in the project.

A similar approach can be taken to the evaluation of any church project: develop a doctrinally based definition, draw implications from the definition, and evaluate the project in relation to the implications.

Incidentally, even if one does not accept McBrien as a theological guide, any D. Min. student faced with the need to develop a definition would be well advised to study the process McBrien uses in developing his definition of the church (1980, pp. 710-721).

Theology as the Basis for an Opinion Survey

The definition of sin as lack of conformity to the divine law does not exclude, but rather necessitates, an inquiry into the characterizing motive or impelling power which explains its existence and constitutes its guilt. Only three views require extended examination. Of these the first two constitute the most common excuses for sin, although not propounded for this purpose by their authors: Sin is due (1) to the human body, or (2) to finite weakness. The third, which we regard as the Scriptural view, considers sin as (3) the supreme choice of self, or selfishness. (Strong, 1907, p. 559.)

The pastor who is concerned about such distinctions may find it useful to see how the members of the congregation regard sin. The D. Min. project could well be devising a questionnaire to see what people consider to be the root cause of sin, and getting members of the congregation to complete the questionnaire. The resulting data would be useful for developing a program of preaching and teaching.

Any such information becomes more interesting and useful when it can be correlated with other information. The other information might be the results of some other questionnaire, or, in this case, the length of time the person has belonged to the church. We would expect those who have belonged a shorter period of time to have theological views more at variance from the pastor's views. If the church has experienced a fairly rapid succession of pastors and the present pastor is fairly new to the congregation, it may be interesting to correlate the questionnaire response with rankings of previous pastors (although there are ethical questions related to collecting such information.)

The construction and validation of a questionnaire to determine how people conceptualize something (such as the root cause of sin) can be an interesting exercise. The most common approaches are to write a series of statements calling for a Likert response, or to write sets of paired statements calling for a forced choice between the statements in each pair. If Strong is your theological guide, a careful study of his logical argument defending his position will give you a good start in writing the statements.

Chapter seven deals specifcally with questionnaire design.

Formulating an Approach to Pastoral Counseling

How does the pastor counsel the person who is worried about a tendency to sin? The answer, while not simple, certainly depends on the pastor's understanding of this basic theological concept.

Segundo (1973), considers St. Paul's complaint that although he knows what is good and desires to do it, he actually does just the opposite (Romans 7:15), an expression of concupiscence, the tendency to sin. Segundo then examines the concept of grace in relation to concupiscence. Concupiscence, he says, restricts liberty if it prevents us from doing what we know to be right. Grace grants liberty, by freeing us to do what is right.

For Paul, then, liberty--not the mere capacity to choose but the positive quality of determining one's own existence for oneself--is the good. Non-liberty--allowing oneself to be taken over by egotism and ease, which is the law that, ruling us from outside our being--is the evil. (Segundo, 1973, p. 27.)

What are the practical pastoral consequences if a minister takes Segundo as a theological guide? Such a minister would attempt to help parishoners achieve liberty. But what does that mean?

Following a careful study of Segundo, the D. Min. researcher would do a careful conceptual study of "liberty," identifying and sorting out the various ways "liberty" has been understood over the centuries. At that point, the pastor will have the tools for offering philosophical guidance to the concupiscent parishoner, helping the parishoner understand what sort of liberty is needed.

In practice, however, the way in which the parishoner receives such philosophical advice will depend on the parishoner's personality structure. So the D. Min. project being suggested here, a project focusing on pastoral care, and assuming the D. Min. student has specialized training in psychology and counseling, would attempt to relate an awareness of a personal tendency to sin to personality structure in such a way as to develop a strategy for counseling in the direction of liberty. It is not a simplistic project, but it can be done, and makes sense if you draw your theological frame of reference from Segundo.

The researcher might have to develop a simple questionnaire to identify those parishoners who are particularly aware of a tendency to sin, or these people might be identified from pastoral conversations and previous pastoral counseling. Sophisticated tests are available that could be used, but they generally identify people with unhealthy anxieties. Such tests might not identify St. Paul, for example. Furthermore, this identification process would not require particularly high validity. The goal is to obtain a sample of people with a greater awareness of concupiscence than would be found in a random sample. If you can find a questionnaire with high validity, use it, but don't let the entire project be consumed by questionnaire construction.

Given this sample of parishoners, interview them about their awareness of concupiscence, how this awareness affects their lives, and how they feel about liberty. Better yet, have a colleague use your interview schedule to do the interview. Also have the people complete a personality assessment test, such as Cattell's 16PF.

Given this information, do an informal "correlation" analysis, sorting the people out according to attitude toward concupiscence and liberty, and then for each group, looking for common personality traits. With the conceptual study of liberty, the interview responses, and the personality information, the pastor should be in a position to offer a theoretical strategy for counseling in the direction of liberty.

Some cautions are in order. (1) As described, this is not an experimental study, and is not intended to be one. It is a theological-philosophical study focusing on pastoral care and employing some empirical information. An experimental study would be much more sophisticated, and might follow this project. (2) A basic assumption here is that the D. Min. researcher has an active interest in pastoral counseling, and has acquired a thorough understanding of the 16PF or any other test that is used.

Helping People Form Attitudes

The theological guide may require that careful evaluation be built into your project. Consider the following from Bloesch (1979):

As we see it, the fundamental dichotomy is not between nature and grace, time and eternity, spirit and matter, but between sin and holiness, light and darkness, God and

83

the devil. (p. 147.)

Having been cast out of the heavenly realm, the devil and his legions have invaded the earthly realm, and he has thereby become the "prince of this world." (p. 149.)

When John refers to the kingdom of the world becoming the kingdom of our Lord and of his Christ (Rev. 11:15), he has in mind the possessions and subjects of the devil, not the devil's government, which will be destroyed. (pp. 149-150.)

Until Christ comes again in glory, the church is engaged in an unceasing struggle with the dislodged powers of darkness. These powers can be vanquished only by the Word of God, not by the sword, though the chaos that they engender in society can be held in check by the sword. (pp. 150-151.)

The writing capsulized in these quotations is clearly establishing a frame of reference. Bloesch is explaining how one should approach the world. How, then, would one who takes Bloesch as a theological guide function as a minister? The immediate suggestion offered by the passage from which these quotations are drawn is that the minister lead a battle against the kingdom of the devil. This is a broad statement, and could take many directions in practice, but it could certainly be a legitimate D. Min. project.

However, if you take it as a D. Min. project, spend a significant amount of time clarifying the theological frame of reference and its implications. In particular, if Bloesch is your theological guide, be careful to understand what he is saying and what he is not saying. In his theological exposition, the focus is on motivation:

The way to regain social relevance in our preaching is to rediscover the social imperatives of the law of God, which certainly form a part of God's word. We need to address ourselves to social as well as personal evils in society when we preach against sin. (p.169.)

84

The Gospel itself is a stick of dynamite in the social structure, and this is why both communist and fascist dictatorships almost invariably place a restriction on its heralds and ambassadors. The Gospel has politically revolutionary implications... (pp. 169-170.)

Our chief motivation for spreading the Gospel, however, is not to overturn oppressive social structures or disturb the existing social order but instead to witness to God's incomparable grace in Jesus Christ and thereby save souls from sin, death, and hell. (p. 170.)

And in his discussion of holiness, Bloesch says,

The call to holiness is also distorted by a certain kind of social activism that confuses kingdom righteousness with social justice and Christian charity with humanitarianism. (p.63.)

It is not necessarily easy to distinguish social activists who take Bloesch as a theological guide from those who take opposing theologians as a guide, or from those who have no conscious theological standard. This means that the D. Min. project would have to be more than organizing a battle. The minister should also do everything possible to see that the "troops" have a fairly sophisticated understanding of why they are fighting, and what the intended ultimate outcome is. The minister who says that it is not necessary for everyone in the fight to be able to intellectualize, so long as the battle is won, will not have taken Bloesch seriously. Bloesch is not a pragmatist.

The key to this project will not be organizational skills (important as they are), but evaluation. Before leaving the study, the D. Min. researcher should have a concrete plan, including questionnaires, for determining at the end of the project whether or not the participants understood the theological frame of reference. In this case, that will be the test of the project's success or failure.

Analysis of Theological Terms as a Primary Problem

A common problem in relating the theological frame of reference to the empirical study is that insufficient attention has been given to operationalizing abstract theological terms.

Gelpi (1978) has written a readable and coherent Catholic charismatic development of theology, Experiencing God. About two-thirds of the way into the book, Gelpi presents 13 principles for Christian education. For one who accepts Gelpi as a theological guide, a worthy D. Min. project would be to use Gelpi's principles to evaluate the local Christian education program. The first task of the paper would be to operationalize the principles and demonstrate that the operationalization is consistent with Gelpi's frame of reference.

For example: "(1) The goal of Christian education from cradle to graduate school is the evocation and charismatic transformation of an adult ego." (p.253.) Two of the key terms here are "charismatic transformation," and "adult ego." They are terms that Gelpi has developed.

> How then does an adult ego come to be charismatically transformed?...first repentance, then the submission of the developing ego to the obedience of faith through habitual openness to the Breath [i.e., Holy Spirit] in shared and personal prayer. (p. 227.)

This brings us closer to an operationalization of the principle. The next questions are, within Gelpi's frame of reference, how does one identify repentance, and how precisely can we identify Gelpi's understanding of shared and personal prayer?

Another question related to the first principle is how the educator "evokes" the "adult ego."

> That environmental, qualitative, perspectival, habitual, and decisive variables condition the waxing and waning of adult ego-consciousness should be clear. Stimulating environments intensify ego-awareness; boring ones stifle it. (p.177.)

This is a hint as to how Gelpi sees the evocation taking place, and it offers a concrete beginning. But a full understanding of "evocation" requires careful study of Gelpi and related writers.

Some of Gelpi's 13 points are fairly concrete and require little interpretation. Others require a great deal of interpretation. But all can be analyzed and operationalized to yield a concrete and relatively objective evaluation schedule.

From this brief example, it should be clear that for some D. Min. projects, operationalization of the theological terms would be the major task of the project.

What is Morality?

Issues of morality are "frame of reference" issues.* The choice of a moral code is intrinsically related to one's frame of reference. (Consider the example of the shirt makers from the beginning of this chapter.) Take Tillich, for example. He denies any absolute moral code:

> The ambiguity of the moral law with respect to ethical content even appears in the abstract statements of the moral law and not only in their particular application. For instance, the ambiguity of the Ten Commandments is rooted in the fact that, in spite of their universalist form, they are historically conditioned by the Israelitic culture and its development out of the surrounding cultures. ... The human reception of every revelation makes the re-velation itself ambiguous for man's action.

---

*   There is another sense in which issues of morality are "frame of reference" issues. This is the sense demon-strated by Kohlberg, Rest and their associates (see chap-ter 6) who have shown empirically that a person's approach to morality is a developmental affair. At different stages of life, people adopt different frames of reference for making moral decisions.

A practical consequence of these considerations is that the moral conscience is ambiguous in what it commands us to do or not to do. . . . The conflicts between tradition and revolution, between authority and autonomy, make a simple reliance on the "voice of conscience" impossible. (1963, pp. 47-48.)

The researcher who accepts this frame of reference (i.e., the validity of absolute moral codes) might do an anthropological study of responses to a moral issue of an issue in social ethics in a congregation, or in several congregations in a community. Or the researcher might try various methods of increasing tolerance for ambiguity in a congregation (cf. Davies, 1982). A pastoral counseling study growing out of this frame of reference might employ a counseling approach clearly congenial to the theological position, and compare its results with people of various personality profiles. Once again, the point is that accepting a frame of refernce should condition the design of an empirical research study.

Example: An Actual D. Min. Project

Theological study convinced Conway (1975) that several contradictory models of the church are operative within the contemporary Catholic church. Out of her study, she characterized three ecclesiological models: "pre-conciliar," "conciliar," and "post-conciliar." She then identified six theological issues in the life of the church that highlight differences among the models. For each of these issues, she identified three areas of practice that would discriminate among the three ecclesiological models (pp. 35-41):

1. The relationship of the church and the world.
   (a) The work, lifestyle and garb of religious women.
   (b) Prayer and church activities.
   (c) Religious vocations vis a vis other vocations.

88

2. God's intentions regarding church structure.
   (a) The function and authority of a parish council.
   (b) Evaluating the performance of the clergy.
   (c) The role of the laity in the church.

3. The church's involvement in social issues.
   (a) The appropriateness of sermons on social justice.
   (b) The role of the laity in social justice ministry.
   (c) The criteria for the distribution of charitable donations.

4. The role of the sacraments.
   (a) The place of baptism within a parish.
   (b) The character of the Sunday eucharist.
   (c) The role of homilies at liturgies.

5. How we come to learn about God.
   (a) The function of law and conscience.
   (b) The educational emphasis of a parish.
   (c) Children and worship.

6. The relationship of the Roman Catholic Church to other Christian churches.
   (a) Ecumenical relationships.
   (b) Intercommunion.
   (c) Validity of Protestant orders.

For each of the six theological issues, she prepared a brief statement representing the position of each ecclesiological model. For example:

1. The relationship of the church to the world.

Pre-conciliar: The church stands in opposition
                  to the world. It is the
                  church's business to convert
                  the world by confronting
                  its evils.

Conciliar: The church and the world
                  are mysteriously related.
                  Each is a part of the other.
                  It is the church's business
                  to challenge the world to
                  be fully human.

89

Post-conciliar: The church and the world cannot
be separated from one another.
It is the church's business
to be in the world, reforming
it, and being reformed by it.

Similarly, for each of the 18 areas of practice
she wrote brief statements relating each area of
practice to each ecclesiological model. The 18 issue
statements and the 54 practice statements were then
formulated into a questionnaire that could give a
measure of the degree to which the people of a parish
accept each of the three ecclesiological models in
both theory and practice.

She surveyed three parishes, and came to some
conclusions about the theory and practice of
ecclesiology that are both interesting and
significant. But the important lesson for us at this
point is that this is primarily a theological thesis,
and only secondarily a sociological one.

Perhaps a reader will find fault with Conway's
theological analysis, but the point remains that a
great deal of clear-headed effort went into the
doctrinal portion of her thesis. It is a good example
of how theological analysis can relate doctrinal
statements to life as it is lived. The same
analytical process could be used in studying other
matters of theological concern.

Teaching and Preaching

In this discussion of theology as a frame of
reference, there has been little mention of using the
theological position as subject matter for teaching or
doctrinal preaching. This oversight has been
intentional.

Since teaching and preaching are two of the most
important pastoral functions, it is certainly
appropriate for teaching or preaching to be the
project. Furthermore, it seems that theological
claims are "meant" to be taught or preached about.
This is why teaching and preaching are by far the most
common forms of D. Min. project. It did not seem

necessary to say more about teaching and preaching in this chapter, because you should have little trouble developing a teaching or preaching project from the writings of your theological guide. Any of the writings we have discussed could be the basis for a teaching or preaching project.

Here, we have attempted, in a simplified way, to describe some other sorts of projects that might be suggested by a theological study.

Theology as a Source of Research Hypotheses

It is safe to say that all theological writing provides a frame of reference. In addition, theologians make assertions of fact that can become research hypotheses.

When the Theologian Makes an Empirical Assertion

The most frequent theological assertions of fact relate to the interpretation of history or scripture. Every beginning theological student learns to deal with such assertions, and we need not be too concerned with them here. But for the sake of comparison, let's consider two factual assertions by Sheldon (1903). The first is an assertion about how the biblical writers understood baptism:

> Cleansing, washing, making new by taking away the old ingrained corruption--this is essentially the typical sense of baptism, as is to be concluded from the natural association of water with purification, from the Old Testament symbolism, and from the tenor of the New Testament references. It is true that Paul in two or three instances associated baptism with burial and resurrection. But, though a considerable number of theological writers, moved in part by a controversial interest, have been inclined to make this representation the standard for New Testament thought, it is decidedly more consonant with the sum total of biblical statements to regard the Pauline

91

sentences as expressive of a secondary
association of baptism than of its primary
and more obvious import. (p.511)

This is a key point in Sheldon's argument about
baptism. It is an assertion of fact. Sheldon claims
that most biblical writers, in fact,   understood
baptism in a particular way. Those who would either
support or quarrel with him would use the appropriate
exegetical tools.

In contrast, as he continues his discussion of
baptism, Sheldon makes, however hesitantly, another
kind of factual assertion:

On the part of children, it [baptism] is a
reminder, as soon as they come to years of
understanding, that they ought not to count
themselves aliens to Christ's family, but
as already having a distinct relation
thereto, which it behooves them to carry
forward to perfection. This relation, it
is true, should not be given too much of
the character of a finality. After
generous room has been conceded to the
charitable assumption that the child
trained in Christian teachings will become
in spirit and in truth a disciple of
Christ, his own choice and line of conduct
should be allowed to determine his standing
as being within or without the circle of
church fellowship proper. Meanwhile, the
consciousness of an already existing
relation to religious society may naturally
serve as a motive for reflection and for
choice in the right direction. (pp.
516-517.)

This same empirical assertion in defense of
infant baptism was presented 63 years later by
Macquarrie (1966, pp. 412-413).

This is an assertion of empirical fact that is
not subject to exegetical verification. It asserts
something about how people, in fact, respond to
baptism, and could be the basis for an interesting D.
Min. project. One way to state the hypothesis would
be:

> Persons baptised in infancy, excluding persons raised in a tradition emphasizing adult believer baptism, will show a greater tendency to become active adult church members than persons not baptised in infancy.

The reason for the exclusion of persons raised in a tradition emphasizing adult believer baptism is because "common sense" suggests that the psychological reaction of persons who think infant baptism is inappropriate might be different from the psychological reaction of persons with no expectation regarding baptism. This "common sense" expectation should be investigated.

The approach to the research is not difficult. Obtain a random sample of adults from each of three groups: (a) persons baptised as infants and raised in a tradition that sees infant baptism as a norm, (b) persons not baptised as infants and raised in a tradition that emphasizes adult believer baptism, and (c) persons not baptised as infants and not raised in a tradition that emphasizes adult believer baptism. Then determine the commitment that each person has to the church, and find the average for each group.

Given this basic approach, the actual research project ought to be a bit more complex. Perhaps group (c) should be divided into two groups: those definitely raised in a tradition that sees infant baptism as a norm, and those raised without a recognition of baptism. Alternatively, one might want to sample various denominations.

The question of how you assess church commitment involves a number of subtleties. For example, a great deal of work has been done on the distinction between intrinsic and extrinsic religious belief. Although there is room for debate (Hunt & King, 1971), it does seem that some (extrinsic) people see their church commitment as benefiting them in come particular way, while others (intrinsic) have faith without regard for whatever personal benefits it might yield.

Apart from the extrinsic-intrinsic variable, King and Hunt have determined that seven different kinds of religious commitment are essentially independent of one another: creedal assent, devotionalism, church

93

attendance, organizational activity, financial support, religious dispair, and orientation to growth and striving. A person pursuing this research project would be well advised to investigate each of these variables.

Then, again, one might study the concept of faith development in relation to baptism (Fowler, 1982).

The point is that the theological essay can provide the basis for an interesting bit of empirical research.

Another Example of Factual Assertion

Tillich makes some assertions of fact about moral attitudes which can become research theses. For example, he says, "In the common judgement, sacrifice is unambiguously good." (Tillich, 1963, p. 43.) This is a testable statement. You could conduct a survey to see what percentage of church people and what percentage of non-church people see sacrifice as good. What about their sacrifice versus somebody else's sacrifice? How much sacrifice is good? The questions can be multiplied and elaborated endlessly.

Theology and Logic

Perhaps more interesting is an assertion Tillich makes about possible attitudes toward the law. Tillich suggests three attitudes that people might hold. First, "the self-deception that [the law] can produce reunion with our essential being." (1963, p.49.) This statement and Tillich's elaboration of it require analysis of the way he employs philosophical terms, but given the analysis, the statement is an assertion of fact. The second attitude "is a resigned acceptance of the fact that [the law's] motivating power is limited. . . . This is the attitude of those who try to obey the law and oscillate between fulfillment and non-fulfillment . . ." (p.49.) The third attitude "combines a radical acceptance of the validity of the law with a complete despair about its motivating power." (p.49.)

For one thing, this is a logically interesting assertion, because it ignores three possible logical categories. Tillich is dealing with two variables, or categories of opinion about the law. One variable has two values, the other, three. The variables are "validity" and "motivating power." The people Tillich is discussing will see the law as valid, but some more than others. The two values of "validity" may be called "a great deal," and "limited." The three values Tillich suggests for "motivating power" may be called "a great deal," "limited," and "none." Then there are six logically possible cases, as set forth in Figure 5-1.

HOW MUCH VALIDITY DOES THE LAW HAVE?

		A GREAT DEAL	VALID, BUT LIMITED
HOW MUCH MOTIVATING POWER DOES THE LAW HAVE ?	**A GREAT DEAL**	I. TILLICH'S FIRST GROUP.	II.
	LIMITED	III.	IV. TILLICH'S SECOND GROUP.
	NONE	V. TILLICH'S THIRD GROUP.	VI.

Figure 5-1. Logical expansion of Tillich's discussion of the Law.

What can be said about the empty boxes in Figure 5-1? Of course a logical possibility does not entail an empirical reality. Maybe there is no person who can be placed in boxes II, III, or VI. But in this case, it does not seem absurd to think that there might be people who could be classified in all six of the boxes. So one possible research study would be to sort people into the six boxes, and then compare them on other variables. For example, Tillich asserts that puritans and pietists will be among those in box I. Use the "Puritanism" and "Pietism" scales on Lee's "Religious Belief Inventory" (Appendix) to check this assertion. Will it be true that people in box I will score higher on these two scales (on the average) than people in the other five boxes?

Another example: Tillich asserts that the law "produces hostility against God, man, and one's self." (p. 49.) You might assess people's hostility toward these three entities in various ways, from a simple questionnaire to a sophisticated psychiatric assessment tool. (Of course this will require a study of the literatrue on hostility.) Is there any difference among boxes in the level of hostility? If so, how do you account for it?

As a third example, compare the people in the six boxes on their attitudes toward current issues in social ethics.

A more sophisticated question is whether the six boxes are the most appropriate way to describe people's attitudes toward the law. The researcher could approach this question by devising an appropriate questionnaire and performing a factor analysis on the responses (see chapter 6). Then see if the factors can be interpreted as matching the six boxes. The researcher might also test to see if well researched psychological variables adequately describe the people in the six boxes.

The reader should note that this brief discussion which suggests at least five separate D. Min. research projects, grows out of a single page in a three volume treatise on systematic theology. So long as theology consists of serious statements about life, theology will suggest research questions.

CHAPTER VI

WHAT SHOULD I OBSERVE?
IDENTIFYING AND OPERATIONALIZING VARIABLES

Identifying Variables

Once we have identified a phenomenon to observe, we try to identify the key variables. Sometimes this is very difficult, and the search for key variables may define an entire academic discipline.

For example, how can you construct a sermon so that people will understand it and respond positively? One of many variables is "structure" or "organization." Another is (the presence or absence of) "humor." Another: "time spent in preparation." The search for relevant variables and the ideal "value" of each variable fills a library.

Sometimes key variables are fairly obvious. An administrative study of the most efficient way to communicate with church members would take into account postage costs as one of the important variables (bulk mail is cheaper than first class, but first class mail might be more widely read).

In any case, once you have determined what you want to observe, sit down and make a list of variables you think might be important. Then review the literature to see if you have missed any variables, and to see how others have operationalized the variables. If you don't do this kind of work, you will waste a lot of time.

Independent and Dependent Variables

Researchers talk about two kinds of variable. "Independent variables" are the things that we can and do control. "Dependent variables" are the things that we observe as a result of our control of the independent variables.

For example, Willis, Feldman and Ruble (1977) did an interesting study of children's generosity. The dependent variable was to be how generous the children were, and the independent variables were

97

circumstances that might influence generosity. For independent variables, they chose sex, age, whether the recipient was a crippled child or crippled adult, and whether the donor children earned money or had it given to them.

The independent variables were easy to define for the research study ("operationalize"). For sex and age, four equal groups of children were used: boys between 5½ and 6 years old, girls between 5½ and 6 years old, boys between 8½ and 9 years old, and girls between 8½ and 9 years old. All were given a choice of giving money to a crippled child, a crippled adult or not giving away any money. And in each of the four groups, half were given some money and half "earned" the money.

Once the independent variables are described, the "operationalization" of the dependent variable becomes more obvious than it would have been if the question were simply "How can you measure generosity?" In this study, each child received 50 pennies. "Generosity" was measured by the number of pennies donated.

Results: Older children (mean = 4.73 cents) were more generous than younger children (mean = .67 cents). Girls (mean = 3.92 cents) were more generous than boys (mean = 1.48 cents). Across both age levels, more was donated to crippled children (mean = 3 cents) than to crippled adults (mean = 2.4 cents). There was no significant difference between those who "earned" their pennies and those who did not.

For another example, Jackson (1961, pp. 47-59) describes an informal preaching experiment he once conducted. He defined two kinds of sermon, called "repressive-inspirational" and "analytic." The "repressive-inspirational" sermon is "characterized by a deliberate effort to repress the unpleasant and irritating in life and in its place emphasize the inspirational." (p. 49.) "The analytic method makes a vigorous effort to explore openly the experience of life, and to discover the inner resources that are available to deal with it realistically and competently." (p. 52.)

For sixteen consecutive Sundays, he alternated these two kinds of sermon, attempting to keep each sermon a "pure" type. He enlisted two congregation members who were experts in group work to help him observe the results. (They did not use any formal tools of observation.) No one but the pastor and the two observers was aware of the experiment.

Among the results they observed:
(a) Numerous and warm comments following "repressive-inspirational" sermons. Few sermon related comments following the "analytic" sermons.
(b) Warm congregational interaction on the church lawn following "repressive-inspirational" sermons. Restrained post-worship interaction following "analytic" sermons.
(c) Much more coughing during "analytic" sermons than during "repressive-inspirational" sermons.
(d) Little pastoral counseling initiated following "repressive-inspirational" sermons. Over 200 hours of pastoral counseling begun in relation to the eight "analytic" sermons.

What were the variables and what are their values in this experiment?

There was one independent variable: "type of sermon." It had two values: "repressive-inspirational" and "analytic." We have noted four dependent variables: "comments following sermon" (two values, "many" and "few"), "interaction on the lawn" (two values, "warm" and "restrained"), "coughing" (two values, "much" and "little"), and "sermon related pastoral counseling" (measured as the number of hours of counseling).

The Need to Operationalize

Words serve to link concepts to reality, particularly in interpersonal discourse. But words are imperfect tools. Precise communication is difficult, and perhaps impossible. One reason for this is that our perceptions are imperfect. We are not certain what "reality" is, so we are not sure what words to use in reference to reality, and we are not sure what reality another person makes reference to in using a particular word.

If research is to have validity, this communication ambiguity must be reduced as much as possible. In order to do this, the researcher must "operationalize" the key concepts in the project. In other words, for the purposes of the research project, the concepts must be given a restricted definition. Such a definition will not include all of the connotations that enable the word to enrich our understanding of the concept, but the operationalized definition should approximate the "every day" concept as closely as possible.

A very important and difficult task of empirical research is to operationalize concepts in such a way that they are precise, but not trivial. If the operationalized definition is too narrow, the research results may be highly "scientific," but useless.

It is my feeling that "operationalize" is an ugly word, and for that reason I argue for its deliberate use. When we operationalize a concept, we damage it in some sense, and use of the ugly word "operationalize" may remind us that we are not simply setting forth an alternative definition, but that we are forcing the word to refer to an altered concept. If we remember this, we can assess the limitations of our research.

We have seen operationalization at work in the examples of research described above. In Jackson's informal study of preaching, the concept of "repressive-inspirational" sermon was operationalized as eight particular sermons preached by a particular preacher. The same is true for the concept of "analytic" sermon. We cannot say for certain what the results would be given a different set of "analytic" and "repressive-inspirational" sermons prepared and preached by another preacher.

As another example of operationalization, consider intelligence. Intelligence is a widely recognized human attribute. Some people are "smarter" than others. But what, specifically, is "intelligence?" Our society has not been able to formulate a specific definition that will tell us exactly what to observe when we look for "intelligence." Instead, we have I.Q. tests which "operationalize" intelligence. I.Q. tests are certainly useful, but they are also controversial, with critics reminding us that they do not measure "intelligence." The reminder is true, and the controversy is important (see Gould, 1981).

Example: Ways to Operationalize "Evangelicalism"

Hunter (1981) has written an article that is quite helpful in the attempt to understand operationalization. He addresses the question of how a researcher might best operationalize the concept "evangelicalism," and in the process reviews how various researchers have approached the problem. The approaches are:

(a) Demographic criteria: denominational affiliation, extra-denominational affiliation, or denominational affiliation in conjunction with one or more attitudinal measures.
(b) Attitudinal criteria: attitudes on various combinations of theological and moral questions.
(c) Theological attitudinal criteria.
(d) Elevating the phenomenon to a higher level of theoretical abstraction and then employing attitudinal criteria to measure this abstraction.

The reader interested in an explanation of any of these four approaches can read Hunter's article. In each case, Hunter cites several examples of research that have employed the particular approach. Finally, he suggests a set of criteria that combine three key theological beliefs and denominational affiliation.

The point for our purposes is to illustrate the problem. In an essay on evangelicalism, an author can offer a definition and elaborate on it. However, in an empirical study in which evangelicalism is one variable, a researcher must have a fairly "tidy" way of deciding either who is and who is not an evangelical, or else deciding to what degree a person is an evangelical. (As a matter of fact, in the case of evangelicalism, the existing research divides people into two groups: either a person is or is not an evangelical.)

Another Example: Operationalizing Mysticism

It is interesting to think about operationalizing mysticism because on first thought, mysticism seems to defy operationalization by its very nature.

However, any time we think analytically about a phenomenon, we approach operationalization. In a sense, philosophers are the first ones to operationalize.

Ralph Hood is a contemporary psychologist who has devoted a great deal of work to mysticism. He began his work by studying a philosophical analysis, Mysticism and Philosophy by W. T. Stace, and developed two instruments to measure mystical experience based on Stace and William James's Varieties of Religious Experience (see Hood, 1975).

Another approach to operationalizing mysticism was taken by Douglas-Smith (1971). He wrote letters to newspapers and to religious societies presumed to be interested in religious mysticism asking for descriptions of mystical experiences. He then screened the responses according to criteria for religious mysticism he had established. Out of 1,024 replies, he judged 249 to be descriptions of experiences of religious mysticism. On the basis of a questionnaire sent to the 249, he eliminated 38, leaving 211 reports which he used in his study.

A somewhat similar approach was taken by Cofield (1965) who collected and analyzed 114 reports of "numinous experience" from residents of Kokomo, Indiana.

"Moral Development" as a Case Study

Sometimes an operationalization is so clear and appeals so well to common sense that it attracts widespread attention and is widely accepted as the basic definition of the concept. Kohlberg's theory of moral development is an example.

Piaget (see Pulaski, 1971 or Leo, 1980, for overview and bibliography) devoted a life time to formulation of a theory of how thought processes develop in children. He proposed a detailed pattern of growth in the way a person explains the world. When this notion of growth is applied to morality, it provides a new way of examining moral development. The notion of moral development has been around for a long time, but prior to Piaget, the emphasis had been on teaching right thinking and right behavior (e.g., Hartshorne, 1932, Ligon, 1939). Piaget's emphasis was on "process," not "product."

102

During the course of his work, he gave a little attention to the notion of moral development (Piaget, 1932), however moral development was not central to Piaget's interests, and his approach to the topic attracted little attention for more than a quarter of a century. Then Lawrence Kohlberg chose the study of moral development as his life work, beginning with a doctoral dissertation in 1959. Key to Kohlberg's work was operationalization of the notion of cognitive moral development.

Kohlberg wrote six brief stories that presented moral dilemmas. In extended individual interviews, he told the stories to people, asked them how the protagonist should respond to the dilemma, and why. The verbatum responses were recorded and analyzed on the basis of a complex set of guidelines. The analysis ignored the person's particular decision in response to the dilemma, and only considered the reasons for the decision. On the basis of the analysis, the person was classified into one of six levels of moral reasoning (Kohlberg, 1981, pp. 409-412). Although the analysis was extremely time consuming, the operationalization was so clear that it generated a great deal of response. Educators especially wanted to know how to raise a student's level of moral development.

Subsequently, work has been done on developing short answer tests that assess level of moral development without the analysis of long interviews (Rest, 1979, Wilmoth & McFarland, 1977, Kurtines & Pimm, 1983). The most widely used short test is James Rest's (1979) Defining Issues Test.

In light of the topic of this chapter, consider what has happened in the recent study of moral development. Kohlberg developed a complex operationalization of the concept of cognitive moral development. As an operationalization, it provided a means of studying a phenomenon that had been previously observed, but had not been clearly conceptualized. This operationalization proved to be so attractive that it became widely accepted as a definition of the essence of the phenomenon of moral development. At this point, it was no longer an operationalization, because an operationalization, by definition, is an approximation.

The next step was to operationalize this new definition, because Kohlberg's interviews were too cumbersome for routine use. The Defining Issues

Test is such an operationalization.

The point of this discussion is not to promote or detract from Kohlberg's theory. Since scholarship is based on open debate, the inevitable reaction to Kohlberg has set in (e.g., Dykstra, 1981, Joy, 1983), and it will be interesting to watch what happens, including extensions of Kohlberg's theory, such as Fowler's (1981) theory of "faith development."

Kohlberg's theory is substantial, and might be useful for your D. Min. project.

Choosing Variables

If possible, your variables and operationalizations should relate your research to research that has been done in the past. Such a link will make your research much more generalizable than it might otherwise be. It will also help assure that your variables are valid. If you want to change accepted concepts and operationalizations, you should accept the burden of proof for your decision.

Your choice of variables and operationalizations should grow out of your literature review and your review of available tests. Many variables are routinely operationalized by using tests and questionnaires. In preference to devising your own test or questionnaire, look for one that has been used before. Given a choice of two equally appropriate tests, choose the one that has been used most frequently.

Of course, other considerations can override the choice of the most popular test. Your choice should be reliable and valid. Your choice should be the best available operationalization of the precise concept you are concerned about.

Your choice should be usable. Does it presuppose too high a level of education? (For example, the "Ways to Live" value questionnaire written by Charles Morris [Robinson & Shaver, 1973, pp. 552-559] presumes a high degree of literacy on the part of the person completing the questionnaire.) Does it take too long to administer? Sometimes a quick survey with very few questions will be the best choice because of time pressure, even though it is less valid than a more comprehensive survey. (For example, standard intelligence tests are quite long. If you need a quick approximation to intelligence, short forms are available, or among adults who are all approximately the same age, you may want to ask how many years of formal education they have completed.)

Of course there are ways to operationalize variables other than by using tests and questionnaires. Webb, Campbell, Schwartz and Sechrest (1966) argue that "interviews and questionnaires intrude as a foreign element into the social setting they would describe" (p. 1), and call for operationalizations that will confirm test and questionnaire results. They describe a wide variety of "unobtrusive measures" that have been used in research studies.

An Exercise in Operationalization

Darwin (1976, p. 22) stated the following eight objectives for his D. Min. research. If they were your objectives, how would you define the variables they imply, and how would you operationalize these variables? For example, in the first objective, "communication within marriage" is specified as the variable. "Depth of communication within marriage" might be operationalized by obtaining reports of the length of each conversation or the topics covered in conversations. But your suggestions might be better.

1. To increase the amount and depth of communication within marriages.
2. To bring couples together to experience mutual support and affirmation.
3. To teach the value of creative conflict in marriage.
4. To teach a Biblical approach to marriage.
5. To teach the pastor's role in dealing with marriage crises.
6. To establish an on going marriage growth group.
7. For me to learn to teach and counsel married couples more effectively.
8. For my wife and me to experience more openness and intimacy with other couples.

Some Variables to Consider

If you want to work with an idea, but can not figure out how to operationalize it, consult professors and fellow students, and look through introductory textbooks in psychology, sociology, anthropology, and communication. Here is a brief miscellaneous list of concepts, mostly drawn from psychology, that I think might be relevant to a large number of potential D. Min. research projects. You may find some of them useful in framing your research.

Socio-Economic Status (SES)

In a study of a parish or of several parishes, you should probably look at this variable, even if it is not a part of your research hypothesis. As an independent variable, along with sex, age and education, it may account for a great deal of variance in your dependent variables.

SES is commonly operationalized by asking the person to specify his or her occupation. The SES level is then scored by refering to a standard list. Miller (1970, pp. 169-199) presents four SES scales.

Intolerance of Ambiguity

I have found this concept very useful in analyzing aspects of interpersonal relations in the parish. For a collection of tests and a bibliography, see Robinson and Shaver (1973, chap. 6).

Locus of Control

This is the way psychologists refer to the degree to which a person makes decisions based on his or her internal values as opposed to relying on external influence. Psychologists have done a great deal of research on this concept, and it has implications for behavior in the parish. In the literature and indexes, you may find this concept refered to as "locus of control," "internal-external" or "Rotter's I-E." Reviews of research on this concept may be found in Robinson and Shaver (1973, chap.4), Sarason and Smith (1971, pp. 404-406) and Jackson and Paunonen (1980, pp. 535-537). Myers (1982) related locus of control to theological concerns.

106

Creativity

This is an intrinsically interesting concept that is very difficult to operationalize adequately. In spite of the difficulty, a lot of effort has gone into the attempt. If you think this might be a relevant variable in your research project, read the research review by Barron and Harrington (1981).

How "Religious" are People?

There is a good chance that a D. Min. project will involve making some assessment of people's "religion." But what does that mean? It depends entirely on what your question is, and the issue is well worth some careful study and thought. Different academic disciplines tend to be partial to different approaches to defining and measuring religious orientation, so do not simply rely on the advise of one advisor.

Most of the research in this area has been done by sociologists who speak of "religiosity." For the most part, religiosity referes to observable religious behavior. For example, Stark and Glock (1968, pp. 14-16) studied religiosity in terms of five categories: belief, practice, knowledge, experience and consequences. (Consequences "identifies the effects of religious belief, practice, experience and knowledge in persons' day-to-day lives." P. 16.) In a more ambitious effort taking the same approach, King and Hunt have tested versions of a questionnaire over a ten year period with more than 2,500 people, and have developed scales to measure 10 categories of religiosity: creedal assent, devotionalism, church attendance, organizational activity, financial support, religious despair, orientation to growth and striving, salience: behavior, salience: cognition, and active regulars. (King & Hunt, 1975, Robinson & Shaver, 1973, pp. 656-662).

King and Hunt's questionnaire is undoubtably valid, and can be recommended for use (in spite of a general caution at the end of their article) so long as their categories are suitable. Their categories will not be suitable for all purposes.

For example, their categories do not deal with motivation, and there is a motivational construct that

107

has been used a great deal: Allport's (1954) division
into "intrinsic" (religious belief and practice for
its own sake) and "extrinsic" (religious belief and
practice for the sake of some non-religious benefit,
e.g., "It's good for business."). Scales to assess
intrinsic and extrinsic religious orientation developed
by Feagin (1964) are included in Robinson and Shaver
(1973, pp. 702-708).

Hunt and King (1971) questioned the validity of
the intrinsic-extrinsic concept in an extensive
article. Apart from whether Hunt and King are right
or wrong about the intrinsic-extrinsic concept, the
concept definitely deals with religious experience in
a manner that is different from the way they deal with
it in their questionnaire. For some research questions, you will want to seriously consider using the
intrinsic-extrinsic concept.

Another approach to religion is to examine the
theological structures in religious belief. Neither
King and Hunt nor Allport are concerned about this.
The best approach to theological belief is Lee's
Religious Belief Inventory (included in the appendix).
This is a collection of scales that measure puritanism, pietism, fundamentalism, humanism, and scientism.
Lee's (1965) contention is that these are independent
dimensions of belief, and that a belief profile
based on dimensions such as these will be more valid
and useful than a simple liberal-conservative theological classification.

Still another question we could ask is how
important beliefs are to people. Campbell and
Fukuyama (1970, pp. 70-72) asked people to rate 12
statements of belief as "true," "probably true,"
"probably not true," or "not true," and defined an
"index of belief orientation" based on the composite
strength of belief. They pointed out some problems
with their index, but the idea of measuring belief
importance could be developed.

If you want to determine how "religious" people
are, you have to consider at least these four options,
all of which are appropriate for research on different
questions.

Dimensionality: A Conceptual Tool

Sometimes an operationalization of a concept
will be invalid because two or more independent phenomena are grouped into the operationalization. If the
phenomena are independent, their association or non-
association may occur in unpredictable ways, so that
we can draw no conclusions from the research.

If two or more phenomena are conceptually related
to a larger phenomenon, but are statistically independent of each other, they are called "dimensions" of
the larger phenomenon. It is helpful to consider the
possibilities of dimensionality in the early stages
of planning a research project. Dimensionality can
profoundly effect the selection and operationalization
of variables.

A Non-Statistical Example of Dimensionality

To illustrate how complicated church growth is,
Donald McGavran (1970, p. 28) suggests we consider
five "lines of distribution" or "axes":

1. Dependence versus independence.
2. Individual versus group conversion.
3. Proportion of total population.
4. Speed of growth.
5. Indigeneity.

Each of these axes is a way of describing a church.
We can think of each of them as a line, and locate
any church somewhere on each of the five lines.

He numbers each axis in equal segments from
one to six. On the first axis, "to qualify for
position 1, a Church would be heavily dependent,
spiritually and materially, on its founding mission.
To qualify for position 6, it would receive no
missionary aid from abroad, carry on all its doemstic
labors effectively, and propagate Christianity inside
and outside its own language area." The second axis
varies from "Church has arisen by pure individiual
decision" to "Church has arisen by pure group
decision." The extremes for the third axis are
"Church forms 1% or less of class or tribe concerned"
and "Church forms 90% or more of class or

tribe concerned." The fourth axis varies from "Church has grown at less than 10% per decade" to "Church has grown at more than 200% per decade." And the fifth axis varies from "Church has been formed in mold of foreign founder" to "Church has been formed in indigenous mold."

In his example, McGavran compares four churches: Iceland (I) in A.D. 1000, Ongole, South India (O) in 1900, the colonial heritage Rhodesian Church (R) in 1952, and an evangelical church in Aracaju, Brazil (A) in 1964. He locates the four churches on the five axes as shown in Figure 6-1.

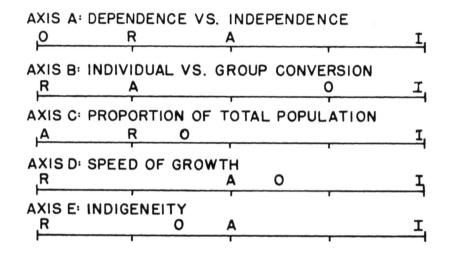

Figure 6-1. Four churches located on five church growth axes (after McGavern, 1970). Used by permission.

We are not concerned with the adequacy of McGavern's approach to church growth, or even with how correct his analysis of these four churches is. The point is that this illustrates the concept of dimensionality, i.e., the concept that we can describe something in relation to several independent axes (or dimensions).

The King and Hunt questionnaire and Lee's Religious Belief Inventory, both mentioned above, provide additional examples of dimensionality. The notion of dimensionality is a powerful conceptual tool.

110

The Source of the Concept of Dimensionality

"Dimension" is a physical metaphor. The idea of "dimension" undoubtably arose when people looked at their world and saw that it had three dimensions: length, width and height.

Twentieth century mathematicians (taking a cue from Descartes) observed that if you mark units of measurement (feet, centimeters or whatever) on three lines, and place the three lines so that they intersect at one point and are mutually at right angles (such as where the walls and floor of a room meet), you can locate any point in space by measuring the perpendicular distance to each of the three lines.

For example a chandelier is five feet north, five feet east, and seven feet up from a particular corner of the room. All three measurements are required to specify its location, but no more than three measurements are required.

The three lines used in establishing such a coordinate system represent dimensions. Measurements on three dimensions can fully describe the location of a point in physical space because each dimension is independent of all others. This notion of "linear independece" can be very helpful for us.

Given an understanding of three-dimensional space (which we can see and touch), we can think about four-dimensional space, five-dimensional space, or n-dimensional space, where n is any positive integer. From the concept of linear independence and a mathematical theorem which says an n-dimensional space is mathematically equivalent to an n-dimensional matrix, mathematicians have developed ways of studying dimensions by analyzing matrices.

A matrix is simply an array of numbers. Here is an example of a three-dimensional matrix:

	column 1	column 2	column 3
row 1	5	5	7
row 2	2.5	3.5	3
row 3	8.0	10	3

111

A four-dimensional matrix would be a 4 x 4 array, and an n-dimensional matrix would be an n x n array.

As it happens, the above matrix represents the location of three objects in a room. Row 1 is the chandelier, row 2 is the back of a chair, and row 3 is the top of a TV. Column 1 is the distance north, column 2 is the distance east, and column 3 is the distance above the floor. Figure 6-2 is a two-dimensional map of the room.

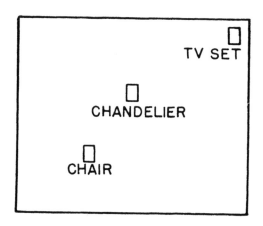

Figure 6-2. Map of a hypothetical room.

The matrix for McGavran's church example would look like this:

I	6	6	6	6	6
O	1	4.5	3	4	2.5
R	2	1	2	1	1
A	3.5	2	1	3.5	3.5

Mathematicians have developed many techniques for manipulating matrices, which allow us to look for dimensions with a certain amount of rigor. The random matrix will not be linearly independent, but we can reduce it to linear independence, and the mathematical manipulation will tell us how many dimensions underlie the test results or other measurements we have. This leads us to a discussion of "factor analysis."

112

Factor Analysis

"Factor analysis" is a statistical technique for examining a set of data to see how many dimensions (also called factors) comprise the data set. The calculations are complex, and the technique was not widely used before research computer centers were established on major university campuses. Factor analysis using a large computer is relatively simple, and it is becoming a common statistical tool.

The computer print-out will give you a matrix in which each factor is a column, and the rows are your original variables. (The variables will typically be individual test items or various tests.) The numbers in the matrix represent the degree of association found between the factor and the variable. These numbers range between "-1" and "+1." "0" indicates no relation between the factor and the variable. "-1" indicates that the converse of the variable is strongly related to the factor. "+1" indicates that the variable is strongly related to the factor.

The print-out will also indicate the percent of variance accounted for by each factor. The first factor will often account for more than half of the variance, with each succeeding factor accounting for less than the one before it. You must decide (subjectively) how many of the factors have practical importance. Often only two, three or four factors appear to be important.

Then you examine the factor matrix and for each factor note the variables that weigh heavily on it. (There is no objective standard for deciding what "weigh heavily" means.) Based on these variables, invent a name for each factor, and write a description of it. You now know something about the dimensional structure of your concept.

A good basic explanation of factor analysis can be found in Jensen (1980, pp. 185-224). Jensen's purpose in writing was to explain (and defend) I.Q. testing, and he felt it necessary to explain factor analysis because of its role in the development of I.Q. tests. Jensen's work has sparked controversy in both popular and academic circles, but his explanation of what factor analysis is is not part of the controversy, and will reward careful reading.

113

If you find that factor analysis may be an appropriate tool for your study, or if you happen to be interested in the I.Q. controversy, you should read Goud (1981, chap. 6). Gould presents a good non-mathematical explanation of factor analysis, and criticizes authors such as Jensen for assuming that factors, which are mathematical constructs, necessarily exist in our world. Gould's concern has merit. When using factor analysis, never forget that you named the factors. However, do not discount factor analysis as a powerful tool for summarizing an otherwise incomprehensible quantity of data.

A more detailed treatment of factor analysis is Cattell (1978). If you decide to work with factor analysis, you will almost certainly need the services of a statistical consultant.

A Sample Factor Analysis Table

The results of factor analysis are reported in tables. Such tables will be meaningless unless you understand a little bit about factor analysis. Explanation of a smaple table should help, even though not all published factor analysis tables will contain exactly the same information. Many published factor analysis tables omit information for the sake of simplicity.

Conte, Weiner and Plutchik (1982) developed a 15-item test of anxiety toward death. Table 6-1 is reproduced as they published it, showing the results of a factor analysis of response to their test.

We first note that the factor analysis is based on 230 completed tests. (Factor analysis will not be valid if the sample is small.)

The left column, headed "item," gives us a brief description of each test item. The authors published the full test in another table in their article.

Note that every item loads on every factor. This is the reason that factor analysis is inherently ambiguous. (It is a technique for describing an ambiguous world.) In the table, test items have been assigned to a factor because they load more heavily on that factor than on the others. Some authors simplify factor analysis tables by not reporting factor loadings below a certain value, such as .30.

Table 6 - 1

Five-Factor Varimax Rotated Factor Solution of the Death Anxiety Questionnaire (n = 230)

Item	Factor loading				
	1	2	3	4	5
Factor 1					
14. With death may be gone forever	.76	.07	.13	.24	-.20
15. Not knowing what to expect after death	.76	-.11	.10	.19	.17
1. Worry about dying	.73	.16	.06	-.02	.06
2. Die before having done everything	.62	.32	-.01	-.02	.12
12. Leaving loved ones behind	.56	.14	.20	.04	.21
Factor 2					
3. Very ill long time before death	-.02	.78	.13	.17	.28
4. Dying may be very painful	.25	.70	.12	.07	.14
5. Others seeing you suffering	.15	.68	.16	.04	.07
Factor 3					
7. Alone when dying	.10	.19	.90	.08	.14
6. Persons most close not there	.23	.20	.86	.17	.10
Factor 4					
11. Buried before really dead	.00	.12	.09	.80	.10
10. Instructions or will not carried out	.11	-.08	.22	.66	.42
13. Not remembered after death	.33	.30	.01	.63	-.22
Factor 5					
9. Worry expenses a burden for others	.18	.18	.05	.09	.75
8. Lose control of mind before death	.05	.24	.16	.05	.70

Note. The percentage of variance accounted for by each factor is: Factor 1 = 29.9%; Factor 2 = 11.6%; Factor 3 = 8.6%; Factor 4 = 7.4%; Factor 5 = 6.9%.

In this case, the authors were fortunate to find that each item was clearly associated with one and only one factor. The factor loading of item 10, which tends to be associated with both factors 4 and 5, might be questioned, but not questioned seriously. Usually in construction of a test via factor analysis, a researcher will find several items that load almost equally on two or more factors. If a pure factor sturcture is important to the study, items that load on more than one factor must be discarded.

The authors report in the note that their five factors account for 64.4% of the variance. This leaves room for other psychological variables to play a large part in explaining a person's anxiety about death.

In this case, the authors do not report "communalities." When these are reported, they are in a far right column headed "h^2". The numbers in that column will show for each item the percentage of variance accounted for by the factors. An item with low communality is irrelevant to the factor structure, and should probably be discarded.

Figure 6-3 shows a graphic interpretation of Table 6-1. Any factor table can be plotted (two factors at a time) in this fashion. A full graphic display of the five factors would require 10 such figures.

Some Examples of Dimensionality

"Common Sense" and Empirical Dimensions

It appears that McGavran's (1970) "church growth" dimensions are for illustration, and not necessarily based on rigorous data. This is a useful approach to any complex topic. Think about the topic in light of whatever relevant knowledge (historical, theological, common sense, etc.) you may have, and identify as many independent factors (or dimensions) related to that topic as you can. This kind of exercise can help you ask appropriate research questions.

The most useful factors, however, are those that have been identified by systematic techniques. The results of any study involving factor analysis are open for discussion, because of the inherent limita-

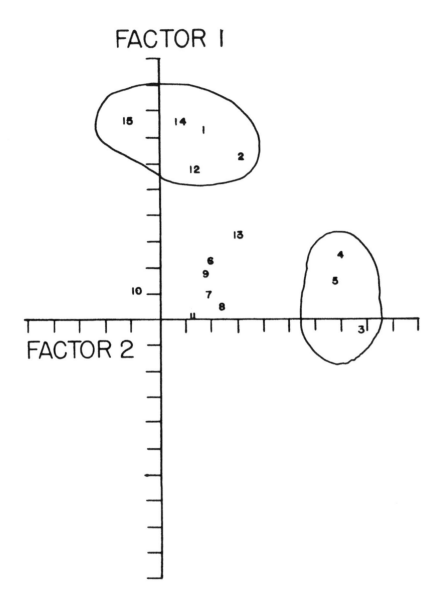

Figure 6-3. A graphic interpretation of the first
death anxiety factors from Table 6-1.

tions of data collection, because factors are seldom unambiguous, and because researchers, with their personal biases, are the ones who name the factors. But even though factor analysis cannot "prove" anything, it can give us some excellent "hints."

A Study of Ministers

For example, as one minor aspect of his Ph.D. dissertation, John Crosbie Carr analyzed questionnaires he had given to ministers, and identified six dimensions which he named and described as follows (1980, pp. 115-119):

1. Power oriented: minister works hard to increase church membership, but is not particularly happy.

2. Administrator-scholar: minister devotes much time to church administration and study, but little time to sermon preparation. Church membership declines.

3. Pastoral servant: minister spends much time in hospital calling, home visitation, and individual counseling, is happy in ministry, does not study much.

4. Senior minister: high salary, long term ministry, high church membership. Minister spends much time in institutional maintenance, little time in pastoral work, is not particularly happy.

5. Pastoral counselor: minister studies and is heavily involved in individual and group counseling. Weddings, funerals and worship services are important. Low priority given to sermon preparation and hospital calling. Worship attendance low in relation to membership. Minister rates self low in effectiveness.

6. Priestly ministry: "minister is involved in ritualized behavior that avoids interpersonal contact."

When we see a list like this, we are inclined to ask, "Which type am I?" But remember, these are dimensions, and any person can be scored on each as having "a great deal" of the quality, "a moderate amount" of the quality, or "not much" of the quality.

Notice that the descriptions of these factors are quite complex. This is typical of empirically derived dimensions. That is why the descriptive names are a matter of researcher judgement and are debatable.

There are two major problems with Carr's list. His analysis is based on 31 questionnaire responses. One cannot make a valid generalization from such a small group. In addition, all of the ministers were of one denomination, male, caucasian, and graduates of the same seminary (Carr, 1980, p. 36). Generalizations from such a restricted sample are dangerous.

Even so, Carr's study gives us a "hint." It is likely that any minister would read Carr's list of factors with a great deal of interest and would find points of identification, as well as points to argue against. At least Carr has provided an interesting pilot study for further research.

For example, a good D. Min. question growing out of Carr's study would be, "What sort of pastoral study (to include time involvement and subject matter) is related to high average attendance at morning worship?" The researcher would want to examine other variables potentially relevant to worship attendance, but this question is certainly worthy.

A Study of Lay People

The King and Hunt questionnaire (Robinson & Shaver, 1973, pp. 656-662, see above) can be useful to you as something to provoke thought, whether you use it as an information gathering tool or not.

When thinking about this questionnaire, keep in mind that it provides a way of profiling members of your congregation. Each of the eleven dimensions is independent of each of the others. If we consider only three of the dimensions, "assent to creedal propositions" (formal belief), "church attendance," and "financial support," and for each of them assign values of "high," "medium," or "low," we would have 27 possible profiles. Figure 6-4 shows some examples. You can probably suggest members of your congregation who would fit each of the 27 profiles.

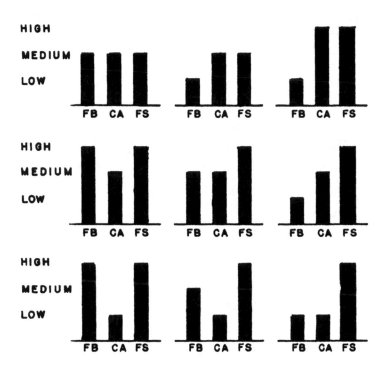

Figure 6-4. Some possible profiles of "Formal Belief" (FB), "Church Attendance" (CA), and "Financial Support" (FS).

CHAPTER VII

WHAT DO PEOPLE THINK?
THE QUESTIONNAIRE

Although this chapter deals with questionnaires,
and chapter 8 deals with tests, the distinction between the two is not always clear. Generally, a
questionnaire is written specifically for a particular
research project, while a test is intended for use in
a variety of studies. Normally a questionnaire deals
with specific or concrete situations, while a test
deals with somewhat abstract concepts. Typically,
questionnaire results are descriptive, while test
results are, in some sense, diagnostic. Note, however,
that all of these distinctions are qualified.

Getting Started: A Horror Story

In July, 1980, the following letter was sent to
a number of religious broadcasters around the country:

> [Researcher's name], who is affiliated with
> [radio station call letters] in [city], and
> I, a minister in [denomination], are involved
> in research regarding the use of radio in the
> area of religious broadcasting. We are look-
> ing to you for information vital to our re-
> search.
>
> Enclosed is a brief questionnaire. We would
> appreciate it if you would take the time to
> fill it out and return it at your earliest
> convenience.
>
> Thank you for your cooperation!

The questionnaire was one sheet of 8½ x 11 paper,
headed "Research Questionaire" [sic]. At the bottom,
in parentheses, it said, "use back of sheet if needed."
Eight questions were evenly spaced on the page:

1. How are you involved in broadcasting?
2. If you were to choose the most influential
   form of broadcasting, what would it be?
3. In the medium, what problems do you see
   right now?

4. What changes would you make to correct the problems?
5. How do you feel about religious broadcasting?
6. What problems do you see with religious broadcasting?
7. What changes could be made to provide better religious broadcasting?
8. What are the "trends of the future" that you perceive for radio and TV?

The first question is all right, but the other seven questions cannot be answered. Read the questions again. List the problems you find with this "research questionnaire." You might never think about sending out anything this useless, but the exercise of criticizing this questionnaire might caution you against making less disastrous, but still bad mistakes in your research.

Some Beginning Tips

Before trying to write a questionnaire, spend some time writing a memo to yourself about what you really want to find out. Then limit your questionnaire to the essentials. Your final questionnaire may be long, but don't make it longer than it has to be.

Given your statement of purpose, determine how you should analyze the information you get. Will you be using statistical analysis? What kind? Will you be asking open ended questions and doing content analysis? Does the information you are seeking break into easily recognized categories? Will you simply tabulate responses, or is a more complex analysis required? There are many things to think about. The point: What form of questionnaire will best meet your need?

Then think about the person completing the questionnaire. How much time can/will this person devote to it? How strongly motivated is the person? Is there any motivation for the person to lie? Does the person have enough education to accurately complete a questionnaire?

Then write a questionnaire that can be answered. The final seven questions on the above "research questionnaire" cannot be answered without further

122

definition. "Influential" for what? "Problems" for
whom? "Better" for what purpose?

Reliability and Validity

How well your questionnaire gives you the information you need depends on how valid it is, and it will
not be valid unless it is reliable.

The literature on testing offers a number of
technical definitions of "reliability." If it should
become a matter of concern in your research, consult
any standard textbook on testing and measurement.
This will be a concern only if your project is to
develop a formal, generalizable evaluation or testing
program.

For most D. Min. research purposes, a questionnaire can be considered reliable if people will give
the same answers (assuming external conditions have
not changed) the second time around. You will probably
not need to test your questionnaire's reliability, but
you must think about it. If a question is ambiguous
(subject to two or more interpretations), no one can
predict which interpretation will provide the basis
for the answer. Ambiguity may arise from the way the
question is written (imprecise language), or from the
way the question is laid out on the paper. I have
been asked to complete forms with items something like
this:

SEX____M____F____.

The problem may be with the typist, not with the
writer, but that does not ease the pain for the person
trying to analyze the data.

Once you are sure in your own mind that the
questionnaire is reasonably reliable, you are faced
with the more difficult problem of "validity." As
with reliability, there are many technical definitions
of validity. For our purposes, a questionnaire is
valid if it elicits the information it was intended
to elicit. There is only one way to find that out.
Try it.

When you think you have a pretty good questionnaire with a well defined purpose, well written and

well laid out, duplicate some copies and ask several
people who are similar to those you will be studying
to fill it out. Then interview them about the experience. Did anything seem ambiguous? Was anything
particularly difficult? Were any words too hard?
Did anything seem silly or superfluous? (This might
affect motivation to answer seriously.) Was it too
long? Did they feel frustrated at any point?

Based on these responses, redesign it and test
it again. Repeat the process until you are confident
that you have a valid questionnaire. (Keep notes so
you can report the validation process as part of your
thesis.)

There is another approach to this problem: use
questionnaires and scales for which reliability and
validity are already fairly well established. Sometimes you can select items from previously used questionnaires. You can find these in journal articles
and books that report questionnaire research results.

A Case Study

Heeg (1979) presented a good illustration of the
need for careful questionnaire design and revision.
The goal for his D. Min. project was personal growth
in preaching ability. To improve his preaching, he
needed to know how people were responding to his
sermons. Here is his report (pp. 44-46):

* * * * * * * * * * * * * * * * *

In order to obtain evaluation of my Sunday
morning's effort which could be measured and compared
to the work of other Sundays, I needed to develop a
framework of objective evaluation. I therefore
developed a Sermon Response Questionnaire which would
indicate progress made in achieving my aims. The first
questionnaire of Feb. 19, 1978 (Figure 7-1), contained
questions which were not specific enough. In our
committee meeting that same Sunday evening, the question arose as to what the first question, "Did the
sermon ring true?" might possibly mean. One member
suggested that if the message does ring true it means
that the pastor is not a fake. I realized that questions 5b "Did you help the preacher preach his sermon
by identifying with the situation or characters in

124

the Bible story?" was less than ideal for a sermon preached on John 4:10,13. Who were parishioners to identify themselves with? Jesus, the woman at the well, or the people from the city of Sychar? The fact that a numerical response was to be given to question 3, "Did the delivery help or hinder the hearing of the pastor's message?" rendered the question ambiguous. One of the younger committee members did not feel comfortable with question 7, "Were you moved by the sermon?" It was also felt that the "Dystopia" heading for the lower scores and the "Utopia" for the higher were not specific enough.

In my attempt to develop a better questionnaire, I studied a number of other questionnaires which had been used by pastors doing in-parish-studies under auspices of the Academy of Parish Clergy. I corresponded with six pastors, although these other forms were not that helpful to me. I needed questions which were clear in meaning and which measured the progress I sought to make. The questionnaire of Sunday, March 19, 1978, (Figure 7-2), contained a weakness in question No. 7, "Did the message open up a new direction of living for you?" One parishioner wrote in his response that Sunday that the question was a bit of a problem to rate. He stated that the question was similar to asking a question such as, "Have you stopped beating your wife?" In future questionnaires, the question was to read, "Did the message draw you to greater commitment and devotion?" After all, the stress of the March 19 message had been this, that we are the recipients of blessings because Christ died for us and that our commitment is an appropriate and desirable response. Furthermore, the previous formulation leads to self-examination, a concern about one's own self, whereas the one about commitment and devotion suggests that the essence of true Christian living is to live before God and for God. The March questionnaire became the first questionnaire of which the results could be indicated on a graph. This questionnaire was the form which was used throughout the year.

Several additions which were of significance for my professional growth were added. The first was the invitation to write a comment in response to question 4b, "How could the delivery be improved?" This was done at the suggestion of a committee member. I amended question 6 in the December questionnaire.

Sunday February 19, 1978

	DYSTOPIA less effective lower score	UTOPIA effective higher score

1. Did the sermon ring true?   1 2 3 4 5 6 7 8 9 10

2. Did the sermon have a single
and unified goal which you
could sense?   1 2 3 4 5 6 7 8 9 10

3. Did the delivery help or hinder
the hearing of the pastor's
message?   1 2 3 4 5 6 7 8 9 10

4. Did the pastor's illustrations
reflect life as you experience
it?   1 2 3 4 5 6 7 8 9 10

5. Did you help the preacher preach
his sermon
   - by active listening?   1 2 3 4 5 6 7 8 9 10
   - by identifying with the
     situation or characters
     in the Bible story?   1 2 3 4 5 6 7 8 9 10

6. Did the message speak to your
life setting, hence to you?   1 2 3 4 5 6 7 8 9 10

7. Were you moved by the sermon?   1 2 3 4 5 6 7 8 9 10

8. Did the message draw you to
greater committment and devotion? 1 2 3 4 5 6 7 8 9 10

9. The message spoke to the follow-
ing needs in my life: 1._____
                           2._____
                           3._____

10. My age bracket is: under 14 __   14-18 __   19-23 __
                                24-40 __   41-55 __   55 & up __

11. Other comments:

Your signature is not required. Please drop in box in
vestibule.   THANK YOU !

Figure 7-1. Heeg's (1979) questionnaire, version 1.

PREACHING RESPONSE QUESTIONNAIRE
Sunday March 19, 1978

<table>
<tr><td></td><td>poor</td><td>weak</td><td>average</td><td>good</td><td>excellent</td></tr>
</table>

1. Was the message a believable
testimony of God's love for you? 1 2 3 4 5 6 7 8 9 10

2. Did the sermon have a single and
unified goal which you could
sense?   1 2 3 4 5 6 7 8 9 10

3. What was the central idea of the
sermon as you understood it?   ---------------------------

4. Did the delivery help the hearing
of the message?   1 2 3 4 5 6 7 8 9 10

5. Were you attentive?   1 2 3 4 5 6 7 8 9 10

6. Was there a fitting (appropriate)
transition from the Bible to life
as we experience it?   1 2 3 4 5 6 7 8 9 10

7. Did the message open up a new
direction of living for you?   1 2 3 4 5 6 7 8 9 10

8. This message spoke to the following needs in my life: 1._____
                             2._____

9. My age bracket is: under 14 __   14-18 __   19-23 __
                          24-40 __   41-55 __   55 & up __

10. Other Comments:

   Your signature is not required. Please drop in box in
   the vestibule.   THANK YOU !

Figure 7-2. Heeg's (1979) questionnaire, version 2.

127

PREACHING RESPONSE QUESTIONNAIRE

	poor	weak	average	good	excellent

1. Was the message a believable
   testimony of God's love for you? 1 2 3 4 5 6 7 8 9 10

2. Did the sermon have a single and
   unified goal which you could
   sense?   1 2 3 4 5 6 7 8 9 10

3. What was the central idea of the
   sermon as you understood it?   ----------------------------

4. (a) Did the delivery (manner of
   speaking) help the hearing of the
   message?   1 2 3 4 5 6 7 8 9 10
   (b) How could the delivery be
   improved?   ----------------------------

5. Were you attentive?   1 2 3 4 5 6 7 8 9 10

6. Was there a fitting (appropriate)
   transition from the Bible to life
   as we experience it?   1 2 3 4 5 6 7 8 9 10

7. Did the message draw you to
   greater committment and devotion? 1 2 3 4 5 6 7 8 9 10

8. This message spoke to the following needs in my life: 1._____
                                2._____

9. My age bracket is: under 14 __   14-18 __   19-23 __
                            24-40 __   41-55 __ 55 & up __

10. Other comments:

Your signature is not required. Please drop in green box
by guest book stand in vestibule.   THANK YOU.

Figure 7-3. Heeg's (1979) questionnaire, version 3.

128

This question had always read, "Was there a fitting (appropriate) transition from the Bible to life as we experience it?" One could interpret the question in wuch a way that the preacher must begin with exposition prior to dealing with the issues of life. Hence, I added "or from life to the Bible?" to the December form, (Figure 7-3). (End of Heeg's narrative.)

Writing Questions

Apart from your own good sense of writing style and logic, and the friendly criticism of your neighbors, one of the best ways to learn to write good questions is to study questionnaires written by others. Beyond that, there is a large literature on questionnaire design. One of the latest "state of the art" reviews is Sudman and Bradburn (1982), a book that is full of useful checklists and concrete examples.

Your first decision is whether a question will be "open-ended" or not. An "open-ended" question has the advantage of allowing the respondent to introduce points of view that may not have occurred to you. Because of this, such questions are particularly useful in pilot studies. But it is difficult to compare "open-ended" responses from different people. In general, most of your questionnaire should consist of questions which give the respondent a choice among a list of possible answers. Follow this main body by a few open-ended questions designed to help you understand the respondent better.

Your biggest problem in actually writing the questions is to eliminate ambiguity. First, will the respondent understand the words you use? Second, will the words convey the meaning you intended?

Sometimes meaning is extremely subtle. For example, consider the two questions, (1) "Do you think the United States should allow public speeches against democracy?" and (2) "Do you think the United States should forbid public speeches against democracy?" It would seem that a person answering "yes" to either question would answer "no" to the other. But it doesn't work that way. In a 1941 study, 10% more people supported free speech when the word "forbid" was used than when the word "allow" was used (Sudman & Bradburn, 1982, p. 137).

Sometimes the ambiguity is not very subtle. In the so-called "double-barreled" question, the respondent is asked two opinions in the same question. For example, "Should our church hire an associate pastor, or should we not hire an associate pastor and keep the youth program at its present level?" About what are people being asked to give an opinion? The notion of hiring an associate pastor, or the notion of expanding the youth program? (See Sudman & Bradburn, 1982, pp. 132-136).

Dillman (1978, pp. 82-83) points out that questions sometimes do not adequately specify what the basis for a response should be. Consider the question:

> To what extent is the obtaining of illegal abortions a problem in this community?
> 1. Not a problem at all.
> 2. A slight problem.
> 3. A moderate problem.
> 4. A serious problem.

Some people might respond "a serious problem" because of their belief that many abortions are obtained, and these produce many medical problems. Others might possess no knowledge about the extent to which illegal abortions occur, but respond with "a serious problem" because they feel it is wrong for anyone to obtain an abortion. (Dillman, 1982, pp. 82-83.)

If you force people to make a choice among various statements, be certain that the statements are independent of one another. The Religious Beliefs of Youth (Ross, 1950) questionnaire violated this principle at several points. For example, item 24 (pp. 43, 235) requests the respondent to choose "the one statement that most nearly describes your position" (your opinion of the church):

1. The church is appointed by God. It is the home and refuge of all mankind.
2. The church is the one sure foundation of civilized life. Every member of society should be educated in it and support it.
3. On the whole, the church stands for the best in human life, in spite of short-comings found in all human institutions.
4. The usefulness of the church is doubtful. It may do as much harm as good.

5. The church is not important today--it doesn't count.
6. The church is a stronghold of much that may be unwholesome and dangerous to human welfare.
7. Other (specify).

Clearly, one who selects (1) would not have selected (6), but is it really possible to make a rational choice between (1) and (2), or between (2) and (3)? The theologically sensitive person might distinguish between (1) and (3) on the basis of (1)'s reference to "God," and (3)'s reference to "human life" as the basis of the church, but will the typical lay person be sensitive to this distinction?

Another approach to this item would be to ask the respondent to respond to each of the six statements on a Likert scale (see below). If you did so and checked correlations among the six responses, you would probably find them to form one scale, with (4), (5) and (6) being reverse items.

It should be said that the Religious Beliefs of Youth questionnaire includes a number of good items. The present discussion is not intended to reflect on the study as a whole.

An exception to the principle of making your statements independent is Privette's "Concept Evaluation Test" (appendix). In this test, people are asked to select the best of several related answers as a way of finding out how well they understand complex concepts ("God," "Christ," "sin," "grace," "salvation," etc.) The choices were carefully developed to reflect a hierarchy of intellectual understanding. This is a much more sophisticated notion than the attempt to inventory a variety of opinions, as in the example we have just considered.

Likert Response: An Approach to Opinion

The Likert response form is a simple and versatile tool for collecting opinions. It consists of a statement to which a person is asked to respond on a five point scale: strongly agree, agree, uncertain, disagree, strongly disagree. For example, here are two items from Lee's Religious Belief Inventory (see appendix).

131

SA A U D SD 1. All preaching ought to include
                an urgent appeal for conversion.

SA A U D SD 2. Christianity is more a philoso-
                phy or a system of beliefs than
                a way of living.

This response form has several good qualities.
It is generally easy for people to decide what their
response is, yet it provides enought alternatives to
satisfy most people. Few people are tempted to respond half way between "strongly agree" and "agree,"
for example. It is economical to lay out. People
have no trouble with a typewritten questionnaire that
asks them to circle their response. It is easy to
score. For example, on item 1, let SA = 4, A=3, U = 2,
D = 1, SD = 0. It takes little time to score an entire
sheet of such items by hand. Note: item 2 was written
to reflect an opposite point of view from that expressed in item 1, so the analogous scoring would be
SD = 4, D = 3, U = 2, A = 1, SA = 0. (We will say
more about this below.)

A less obvious advantage of Likert responses is
that for practical purposes they can be treated statistically as providing "interval data." We will
briefly explain what this means in chapter 9. At this
point, it is enough to say that you can use any
statistical technique in analyzing interval data.
This is not true for data provided by some other
questionnaire forms.

A caution: you will sometimes see questionnaires such as this with the "undecided" option left
out. This is both philosophically and psychologically
unwise. Philosophically, we are sometimes truly undecided on issues, and the questionnaire author who
tries to force a decision out of us will get an invalid response. Psychologically, even if we have an
opinion, we may not want to reveal it, even anonymously. In such a case, the "uncertain" response
provides a place to "hide," and the researcher should
respect this need for a "hiding place." There is
also a statistical consideration. If it is true that
there is a psychological neutral point between "agree"
and "disagree," not providing for a response at this
point will impair the "interval" quality of the data.

Another caution: questionnaires such as this
sometimes substitute "no opinion" for "uncertain."

These terms are not synonymous, and "uncertain" would seem to be the more appropriate choice.

Scaling: Two Questions Are Better Than One

The above two items from Lee's Religious Belief Inventory are examples from one "scale" in that inventory. A scale is a set of items which all relate to a single concept or opinion. The above two items are from an 8-item "Pietism" scale. In the 8-item scale, a highly pietistic person could score 32 (4 times 8), and a person with no pietistic leanings might score zero. Any score in between is possible.

In writing his scales, Lee worked to develop four items phrased positively and four items phrased negatively in each scale. This was done to counter "response bias." Most people will tend to agree with anything they hear or read (and some people will tend to disagree with everything!).

A scale such as this provides for more subtle gradations of opinion than does a single item, because responses on several items will tend to compensate for an idiosyncratic response to one item. You should use scales rather than single items whenever possible.

If you want to test several kinds of opinion, use several scales, and arrange them in random order in a single questionnaire. This will force people to respond individually to each item (decreasing "response set"), thus increasing the validity of the responses. People will also be more willing to complete one comparatively long (but not unbearably long!) questionnaire than several short ones.

For example, if you use Lee's Religious Belief Inventory, take the 48 items and "mix them up" in random order. If some of his scales are not relevant to the question you are researching, leave them out. If you have other scales that are also relevant to your question (perhaps the Purpose in Life test, Phillips, 1980), add them to the mix in your questionnaire. You may also want to include some individual items (not part of any scale) in the questionnaire. These items will tend to be relatively factual, such as:

SA A U D SD 1. Personal problems made my mind wander today.

133

The first couple of items in such a questionnaire should not be part of any scale, but should be
"dummies." People seem to need these for practice, to
get into the rhythm of making such responses.

Making a Scale: Sermon Response

The one thing we require of items in a scale is
that they elicit a smilar response. That is, that
they all measure the same kind of opinion. We assume
that if there is a high statistical correlation (see
chapter 9) among the scale items, they are measuring
one opinion. This assumption is particularly reasonable if the items have been carefully written by
knowledgable people who intended to write a scale.

In 1978, I was pastor to two small rural congregations, including people from all age groups. Few
of the people had formal education beyond high school,
and most of them were employed in industry in a nearby city and worked part time operating small farms.

I decided to study the response to sermons I was
preaching. There were several aspects of the study
which are not relevant at this point, but one part of
the study involved writing a sermon response scale.
I wrote eight statements about sermons, half positive
and half negative:

SA A U D SD 1. I don't know what the point of
                sermon was. (SD = 4)

SA A U D SD 2. The sermon was spiritually up-
                lifting. (SA = 4)

SA A U D SD 3. I would like to study the scrip-
                ture the minister preached
                about. (SA = 4)

SA A U D SD 4. When I thought the sermon was
                finished, the minister kept on
                talking. (SD = 4)

SA A U D SD 5. I've heard the same thing in
                sermons too often. (SD = 4)

SA A U D SD 6. I disagree with most of the
                sermon. (SD = 4)

SA A U D SD 7. The sermon was thought-provok-
                ing. (SA = 4)

SA A U D SD 8. The sermon made me realize I
should change something in my
life. (SA = 4)

Once I had written them, I thought they looked
like they ought to form a scale, so I went ahead with
my study (intended both to improve my pastoral work
and to be a "pilot" study for a larger project which
may or may not ever get done.)

The first week, I explained the project and the
response form, and then for six weeks I included
response forms in the worship bulletin and asked that
they be deposited anonymously in a box at the exit.
At the end of six weeks, 124 usable questionnaires had
been returned. The maximum returned on any Sunday was
29, the minimum was 14.

Based on these 124 responses, the items do seem
to make a scale. The correlation coefficients calculated between any one item and the mean (average) of
all of the items were fairly high (see Table 7 - 1).
This suggests that any one item elicits a response
similar to the average of the responses on all of the
items.

Table 7-1

Correlations Among the Response Scale Items

	6	7	8	9	10	11	12	(mean of items 5-12) "response"
5	.479	.357	.469	.389	.318	.353	.269	.519
6		.440	.305	.474	.258	.221	.272	.677
7			.313	.495	.272	.326	.487	.705
8				.405	.133	.132	.121	.597
9					.269	.334	.297	.700
10						.282	.256	.601
11							.315	.430
12								.583

Two cautions: (1) it would have been better to calculate the correlations between "1" and the mean of "2" through "8," between "2" and the mean of "1" and "3" through "8," etc. (2) since this "sermon response" scale has been used only once, and with a small sample, it should be used with the understanding that it might not "hold up" in another setting.

Not all attemps at writing scales are successful. I once served as a consultant in an evaluation of a U.S. Army weight control program. I wrote some items I hoped would make a scale, including:

SA A U D SD 1. I am glad I have a chance to attend this weight reduction clinic.

SA A U D SD 2. I do not need the weight reduction clinic because I can lose weight any time I want to.

SA A U D SD 3. The Army should not be concerned with a person's weight unless it interferes with assigned duties.

All of the items clearly formed a scale except for the one given here as item 3. All of the items except for item 3 focused on the person, while item 3 focused on the institution, and, for whatever reason, item 3 did not correlate well with the mean of the other items.

When this happens, if you are writing a scale for wide use, you may want to replace the "poor" item and test the scale again. In most cases, however, you simply don't include the item that failed to correlate in your calculations.

Question Formats

Once you have written the qeustions, you still have to design the questionnaire. The task is important enough that you should not leave it to someone else. If the format is difficult to read, the validity of the questionnaire will be reduced.

The best way to judge a format is to pre-test it, but here are some general suggestions drawn form Sudman and Bradburn (1982) and Dillman (1978):

1. Number your questions:
2. Don't continue a question from one page to the next.
3. Use a clean, simple format. Don't crowd the questions.
4. Use upper and lower case letters for the question, upper case letters for the response.
5. Do not put open-ended questions at the beginning of a questionnaire.
6. Provide directions for how to answer, even when it seems obvious.
7. Use a booklet format (both sources advise this).
8. Require only one task for each question.
9. Use a vertical format.

Suggestion number 9 is perhaps the most frequently violated, yet both sources stress this point. The horizontal format is like this.

Give your present marital status:
____never married, ____married, ____separated, ____divorced, ____widowed.

A page full of questions formatted like this can be confusing and discouraging. The vertical format takes more paper, but is easier for the respondent and for the person who tabulates the data:

Give your present marital status:

_____ never married.

_____ married.

_____ separated.

_____ divorced.

_____ widowed.

Maximizing Survey Response

If you are doing a survey, you want to get the maximum possible response. To do this, you must plan ahead. You will probably not be able to afford teams of interviewers or banks of telephones, so it is most likely that you will conduct a mail survey. Typical response to a mailed questionnaire is 30%, and it is not difficult to find published studies based on such

137

responses. Follow-up mailings will increase this percentage, and you may want to consider phone calls or
home visits to increase the response even more.

Research studies in survey design often contra-
dict one another, but there are some definite suggestions to be made:

1. Most important, plan your survey. Design
    the questionnaire carefully. Select your
    sample carefully. Structure follow-up
    mailings into your initial plans. Budget
    adequately for printing, postage and
    secretarial help.
2. Use a clean, simple, easy to read format
    for your questionnaire.
3. Treat the respondent courteously. Include a
    postage paid return envelope. Individually
    address each envelope. Mail the questionn-
    aire first class. (Some studies show a
    better response when a current commerative
    stamp is used, instead of an ordinary stamp
    or postage meter.)
4. Explain why you need the information. There
    are so many advertising appeals disguised
    as opinion surveys that people may not trust
    your request.

Beyond this sort of advice, Dillman (1978) offers
detailed instructions for getting an average response
of 74% (p. 21). He calls his system the "Total Design
Method" (TDM). TDM specifies how the questionnaire is
to be printed (a booklet, 6 1/8" x 8 1/4", elite type-
writer type, reduced to 79% of original size) (p. 121),
and suggests how to establish the sequence of questions. TDM gives careful consideration to writing the
cover letter for the original and follow-up mailings.
TDM specifies three preplanned follow-up mailings, the
third being sent certified mail. And TDM even specifies how the mailings should be folded and put into
the envelope.

You may not feel that your survey warrents the
time and expense required by TDM, but in any case, if
you are planning a survey, Dillman's book is worth
reading for its many practical hints.

CHAPTER VIII

CAN I BE OBJECTIVE? TESTS AND OTHER
TOOLS FOR SYSTEMATIC OBSERVATION

In this chapter, we use the word "test" broadly.
As was mentioned in the last chapter, there is not
always a clear distinction between tests and questionnaires. With both tests and questionnaires we have a
concern for reliability and validity. In other words,
care should be exercised in choosing or constructing
them.

Where to Find Tests

A fairly large number of tests useful for the
study of religious "attitudes" and knowledge are cited
in a review paper I wrote several years ago (Davies,
1977). This paper is readily available through the
ERIC document system.

You will probably have to develop your own tests
of knowledge. A number of efforts have been made at
developing standardized Biblical knowledge tests, but
there are problems with almost all of them. Besides
that, they are not readily available today. There are
currently no standardized tests of religious knowledge other than Biblical knowledge.

The best compilation of what are broadly called
"attitude tests" is Robinson and Shaver (1973). This
book includes 127 "scales" that have been used in
published research. They deal with constructs such
as "self-esteem," "locus of control," "alienation."
"authoritarianism," "values," and "religious attitudes."
These tests are all fairly short and are easy to score
and interpret. If you need an attitude test for your
project, Robinson and Shaver is the first place to
look.

Three other useful compilations of tests are
Miller (1964), Shaw and Wright (1967) and Bonjean,
McLemore and Hill (1967).

In addition, you will find references to tests
as you carry out your literature review. In some

cases, your search for the appropriate test will
involve correspondence with the authors of published
research. Their addresses are frequently listed in
conjunction with journal articles.

Standardized Tests

Most of the tests considered in this chapter are
research instruments, not intended for precise diagnostic work. Their purpose is quite different from
a standardized diagnostic test such as the Minnesota
Multiphasic Personality Inventory (to name one such
test with which you are probably familiar). Standardized tests are purchased from test publishers, while
research tests are often reproduced by the researcher.
Distribution of standardized tests is often limited
to members of the American Psychological Association.
A faculty member who belongs to the A.P.A. can help
you at this point. Some standardized tests are
difficult to administer, score and interpret, and
require special training.

The best list of standardized tests is the series
of Mental Measurements Yearbooks (e.g. Boros, 1978).
These books, which are not annuals, in spite of the
name, not only give information about the tests, but
include detailed critical reviews of some tests.

Some Potentially Useful Tests

Religious Belief

Lee (1965, see appendix) contends that theological belief is more complicated than simply "liberal"
or "conservative," so he developed scales to assess
levels of "puritanism," "pietism," "fundamentalism,"
"scientism," and "humanism," using historical definitions of these theological movements. His Religious
Belief Inventory is particularly useful with church
groups, while the less closely refined measures of
liberalism-conservativism are more useful with the
general public.

Lee's approach to belief as a theological construct is quite different from the approach of King
and Hunt (1975) that studies religious belief in terms
of behavior. If your project involves studying

140

religious belief, you will need to consider carefully what you intend to study, so you can choose the most appropriate test. (See the discussion of reliogisity in chapter 6.)

Ames (see Hart, Ames & Sawyer, 1974) has developed a Philosophical Belief Inventory that provides scores for "idealism," "realism," "pragmatism," "phenomenology" and "existentialsim." Another test, the Ross Educational Philosophical Inventory, provides scores for "idealism," "realism," "pragmatism," and "existentialism." It is available from the author, Colvin Ross, School of Education U-33, University of Connecticut, Storrs, Connecticut 06268.

Purpose in Life

You may want to find out how "meaningful" life is for the people in your study. A simple test which has been used a great deal and seems to be valid is Crumbaugh and Maholick's Purpose in Life Test (Phillips, 1980). This test consists of 20 statements to which people respond on a Likert scale. An example is, "I am usually exuberant, enthusiastic." The test was devised to operationalize Victor Frankl's notion of "meaning" and "existential vacuum."

Crumbaugh (1977) has also developed a related scale, the Seeking of Noetic Goals test, that you may want to examine. This test measures strength of motivation to find meaning in life.

Your may also want to look at the Life Attitude Profile (Reker & Peacock, 1981), designed to measure purpose in life along with other related variables.

Moral Development

Level of "moral development" is an interesting variable to investigate in relation to a large number of phenomena such as response to sermons, response to counseling, involvement in the parish program, or involvement in the larger community.

As we noted in chapter 6, there are a number of short answer tests of moral development (Wilmoth & McFarland, 1977, Kurtines & Pimm, 1983), but the most widely used is the Defining Issues Test. In his book, Rest (1979) gives a full explanation of the background and use of the test. The Defining Issues

Test is included in Rest's appendix. The book is "must" reading if you want to test level of moral development.

Ministerial Job Satisfaction

The Ministerial Job Satisfaction scale, developed by Glass (1976), has not been widely used, but it is so potentially useful for certain D. Min. research topics that it seems worthy of mention here.

"A Study of Values"

This test, written by Gordon W. Allport, Phillip E. Vernon and Gardner Lindzey, is in its third edition, and has been used very widely since its introduction in 1931. There are extensive bibliographies and reviews in each Mental Measurements Yearbook since the third one (cf. Buros, 1978, entry 686, pp. 1100-1104).

"A Study of Values" measures an individual's commitment to six "values": theoretical, economic, aesthetic, social, political and religious. These values were initially identified in a theoretical study, and one may question the adequacy of this as a definitive list of values. However, since the test has been so widely used (over the years, Buros has collected a bibliography of 1,027 published articles that used the test), it may be good to use this test in preference to another measure of values unless there is a particular reason to use the other test. If you use the popular test, you can compare your results with previously published findings.

Semantic Differential

A powerful technique for quantifying attitudes toward almost anything is the semantic differential. The standard work on the technique is The Measureent of Meaning (Osgood, Suci & Tannenbaum, 1957). Another valuable reference is Snider and Osgood (1968), which includes a large bibliography of semantic differential research studies. After studying the earlier work, you may want to read Osgood, May and Miron (1975).

Those who use the semantic differential technique assume that people respond to concepts in complex ways, and that we can describe affective response in metaphorical terms. To use the technique, you select a concept and select a series of adjective pairs such as "good-bad" and "powerful-powerless." The words in each adjective pair are opposites.

For the heading on the response form, state your concept. Write the adjective pairs below the concept with seven spaces between the words in each pair. Alternate the order of the adjectives so that sometimes a positive adjective is first, and sometimes a negative is first. The form will look like this:

Our Food Pantry Project [this is the concept]

nice ___:___:___:___:___:___:___ awful

powerless ___:___:___:___:___:___:___ powerful

alive ___:___:___:___:___:___:___ dead

The respondent is to mark a space (not circle a colon) for each pair of adjectives, indicating the degree to which he or she considers the concept to be nice or awful, powerful or powerless, alive or dead. Note that the spaces should be aligned in columns to help the respondent judge where to make check marks.

The adjectives should be chosen so they do not have a literal denotative meaning in relation to the concept. The goal is to elicit metaphorical responses which will reflect affective response. For example, it would not be appropriate to ask for a response to the concept "stove" as hot-cold, but it would be appropriate to ask if a sermon is (metaphorically) hot or cold. Such a response to the sermon would help reveal attitude.

Over the years, Osgood has claimed that there are three major dimensions of attitude or affective meaning revealed by the semantic differential technique: "evaluation," "potency," and "activity." As you will recall from chapter 6, dimensions are independent. Thus, for example, two concepts may be highly "potent," while one is evaluated as "good" and the other, is evaluated as "bad."

As an exercise in thinking about these three dimensions, think about the twelve disciples and how they might fit in the categories of Figure 8-1. Do you agree with the descriptions of Peter, Judas, and Thomas as they have been entered into Figure 8-1?

EVALUATION	GOOD		BAD	
POTENCY	STRONG	WEAK	STRONG	WEAK
ACTIVE	PETER		JUDAS	
PASSIVE		THOMAS		

Figure 8-1. A Dichotomous illustration of Osgood's three man factors, as they might be used to categorize the Disciples.

Osgood suggests the following adjective pairs to assess evaluation, potency and activity responses (Osgood, May & Miron, 1975, p. 172):

Evaluation: nice-awful
good-bad
sweet-sour
helpful-unhelpful

Potency: powerful-powerless
strong-weak
deep-shallow
big-little

Activity: fast-slow
young-old
noisy-quiet
alive-dead

To score the semantic differntial, assign 7 to the space closest to the positive adjective, 1 to the space closest to the negative adjective, and the intervening numbers to the other spaces. For each factor (evaluation, potency, activity) calculate the mean of the adjective scales.

Not all researchers have found a neat evaluation-potency-activity factor structure, and some researchers have developed special sets of adjective pairs for particular purposes. Smith (1959) studied the semantic differential in relation to speech related concepts. If your project deals with preaching, you may want to read his article. (In 1978, Smith published a very complicated method of studying response to speeches.)

If you have access to a large computer, it is a good idea to perform a factor analysis on your semantic differential data. Such analysis can yield new insights into the object of study. However, the semantic differential technique is quite robust, and the data can be interpreted with reasonable validity assuming the factor structure as Osgood says it would be.

The semantic differential technique is an important tool for pastoral research because the form is easy for people to complete, it is fairly easy to score, it can be applied to all kinds of programs, projects, events, circumstances and personalities, and it gives a more satisfactory response than a one-dimensional question about how well the respondent "liked" the object of evaluation.

Group Tests

In a church, your concern is sometimes more for the group than for individuals. How is the group functioning? The literature on this subject will be indexed under the headings of "organizational development" or "organizational climate."

One student of organizational climate studied an inner-city school by spending a year taking photographs of daily life in the school. The collection of pictures became his doctoral dissertation (Sexton, 1972, 1973)!

Schmuck et al. (1972) published a number of instruments for gathering data about communication, group goals, conflict, perceptions of meetings, decision making and other aspects of organizational climate.

Herb Miller has developed the "Miller Multiphasic Congregational Personality Inventory" (MMCPI), a set of 72 true-false questions to be answered by church board members and sent to Miller for scoring and interpretation. The 72 questions measure 12 congregational characteristics. I have not seen reliability or validity data on this test, but it has enough potential use that it seems worth mentioning. Investigate it before you use it. Write to the National Evangelistic Association, 2323 Broadway, Lubbock, TX 79401.

Another project to assess the climate of congregations and how satisfied members are with their church is being developed by Kenneth Pargament and his colleagues. They call it the "Congregation Development Program." For information, write to Kenneth Pargament, Ph.D. or Willaim Silverman, Ph.D., Department of Psychology, Bowling Green State University, Bowling Green, Ohio 43403.

Content Analysis

"Content analysis" is a formal way of addressing the question, "What, in fact, does a narrative say?" Content analysis can be applied to any discourse: newspaper articles, minutes of meetings, transcripts of interviews, fiction, or any other discursive message.

The notion underlying content analysis is simple. You seek agreement on the structure of the message among members of a panel of competent judges after each has performed the same formal analysis of the message. The analysis will deal only with the relatively objective aspects of the message, that is, aspects which one might reasonably expect experts in a particular field to agree on.

Content analysis developed as a tool for studying journalism. A typical early content analysis study, published in 1930, examined the amount of foreign news in morning newspapers. One would expect to find a high correlation among the judges in such a study. There would likely be a lower correlation among the judges if the question being studied asked whether references to something were favorable or unfavorable, because of the ambiguity of sarcasm. Some judges might see a passage as sarcastic, while other judges would not see it that way. Still more difficult would be a content analytic study of "Values in Mass Periodical Fiction, 1921-1940" (Johns-Heine & Gerth, 1949).

A D. Min. researcher might use content analysis to study the incidence of some counselor characteristic or some client characteristic in pastoral counseling verbatums, or might analyze church newsletters to see what sort of programming has been carried on in the church. If a research questionnaire included some open-ended questions, content analysis should be used

146

to determine objectively how the people responded. A
brave pastor might learn a great deal by submitting
sermons to a set of judges for analysis of pastoral
sensitivity or theological themes.

A typical first reponse to a content analysis
problem is that the researcher is competent to do such
analysis without help. Indeed, the researcher may
serve as one of the judges, but additional judges are
needed for the sake of objectivity.

When you design a content analysis study, begin
by establishing your coding categories. The coding
categories must not overlap one another, and must ex-
haust the logical possibilities of the larger unit. In
other words, coding categories are values of a variable.
The worth of your study will depend on the adequacy of
your categories. The categories should provide you
with the answer to the question you are asking, so put
careful thought into defining your categories.

Next you establish the "unit of analysis." In
doing the analysis, a judge will be asked to classify
each unit of analysis into one coding category. If
the unit is large (for example, if a unit is an entire
sermon), it may be hard to decide which of several
categories it best fits. Because the meaning of many
statements depends on the context, some content analysis studies also specify a "context unit" as the
largest context a judge may examine in coding the unit
of analysis.

Once the categories and unit of analysis are
specified, the judges simply make check marks on coding
sheets provided by the researcher. The researcher then
counts the check marks.

If you think content analysis has a place in
your research, read Berelson (1952) for specific information. You can find more recent material on content
analysis, but Berelson's book is still a good basic
guide. Budd, Thorp and Donohew (1967) included a 309
item annotated bibliography of content analysis studies
in their book. Fowler (1981, cahpter 22) provides an
informal example of "content analysis" of a psychological interview.

Interaction Analysis

"Interaction analysis" is a method for systematically observing the kind of communication that takes place in a group. It requires a pre-determined set of communication categories and one or more trained observers. Observers watch the group at work and every few seconds note who is talking and what category the talk is. The results can help a leader understand the group, and can also be used to train the group to function more effectively.

Interaction analysis began as a way of studying school classrooms and helping teachers to be more effective. (cf. Amidon & Hough, 1967. Ned Flanders is one of the key people in the development of interaction analysis.)

William Bass (1977) developed an interaction analysis procedure based on Flanders that is particularly useful for the study of church groups. We quote his description with minor changes (pp. 58-63):

* * * * * * * * * * * * * * * * *

The procedure is a simple one. The observer sits in the room where the small study group is meeting so that all the participants in the group can be seen and heard. At the end of each three-second period, he/she decides which category best represents the communication taking place at that time. the number of the category is then entered on the coding sheet in the column under the name of the person doing the talking. While the observer is writing down this category number, he/she is already assessing the communication taking place in preparation for the next coding entry. The tempo of coding should remain steady at about twenty to twenty-five observations per minute. The result will be columns of numbers (one number on each line of observation time) proceding from top to bottom down the coding sheet (Figure 8-2). If anything happens which disturbs the interaction of the group, e.g. a telephone call, then that should be noted in the margin beside the unit of time. This method of observation and coding of the interaction should continue for the duration of the group's meeting. The observer should also make note of the seating arrangements during each session, and particularly, how those change (if they indeed do) during a session, or from

148

session to session. Eagh page of the coding sheets
should be numbered consecutively during each session.
If these procedures are followed, then the coding
sheets will reflect the participation of the individual
members of the group, the outside events which dis-
turbed the interaction of the group, and the sequence
of the amount and type of an individual's interaction
within the group.

The categories which I (i.e., Bass) developed to
analyze the interaction of the small group is a
system of eleven numbers. This system is outlined in
Table 8-1. Three of the categories reflect an "Other
Person Orientation" in verbal communication, while
three categories reflect an impersonal, or "Neutral
Orientation," and four categories reflect a "Self
Orientation" in verbal communication. (At the meeting
of the first session of the small group, there were
only three "Self" oriented categories. At that meeting
it became quite obvious that another category reflect-
ing a deeply personal level of sharing information
about oneself was needed. Therefore category 9+ was
added to the system.) The eleventh category classi-
fies pauses in the group's interaction, i.e. periods
of silence, or periods of confusion and/or noise
during which time the interaction of the group is
undistinguishable.

Within each of the three major groupings of the
system there is a category which represents an interaction of concern, an interaction of acceptance, and
an interaction of a neutral nature with regard to that
larger grouping. In other words, category 1 reflects
concern for others by relating to them on a basis of
accepting feelings and of being free to express feelings, while category 7 reflects concern for self by
relating to others in an offensive manner, i.e. by
trying to make them conform to one's own standards, or
behavior. Category 4 reflects a concern in neutral
matters by questions about content or procedure, and
thus keeping the interaction away from either "others,"
or "self." In the same way category 2 reflects acceptance of others by praising and encouraging them,
while category 8 reflects the acceptance of self by
justifying one's own authority through an outside
source as a means of support. Another way of looking
at category 8 is that having to justify one's own
authority demonstrates a need for acceptance by the
individual talking. The neutral categories in each
grouping demonstrate non-threatening interactions,

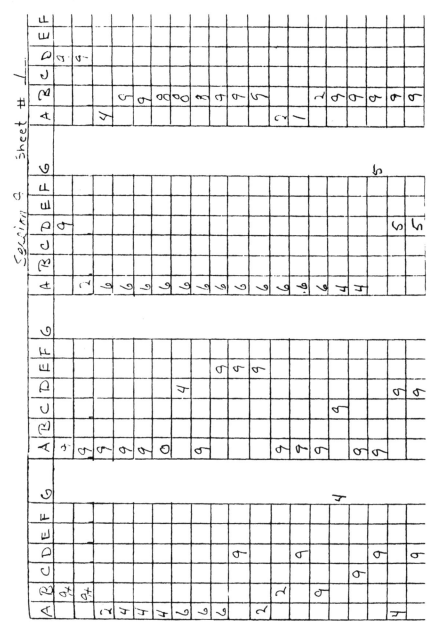

Figure 8 - 2.   Interaction Analysis Coding Sheet.

150

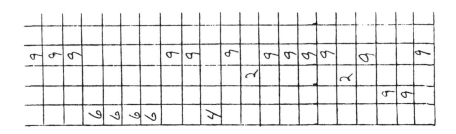

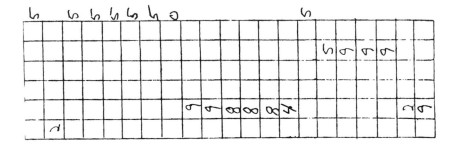

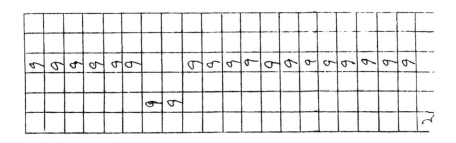

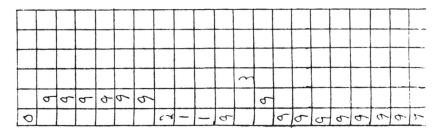

Figure 8 - 2. (continued)

Table 8-1

Categories for Coding Interaction of Small Study Group

	C*	1. ACCEPTS OR EXPRESSES FEELINGS: Accepts and clarifies the feeling tone of group members in a non-threatening manner. Feelings may be positive or negative. Also, expressing, predicting or recalling feelings are included. E.g. "I have been worried about..." or "What you are experiencing is..."
OTHER PERSON ORIENTATION	A	2. PRAISES, ENCOURAGES, OR LOVINGLY CHALLENGES: Praises or encourages group members action or behavior which includes loving challenges. Nodding of head or saying "Uh Huh" or "Go on" are included. E.g. "That is really good", or "Please continue."
	NT	3. TENSION RELIEF: Stories, jokes, etc. which relieve tension but not at the expense of other group members.
	C	4. QUESTIONS ON CONTENT: Asking questions about content or procedure. E.g. "What happens now?" or "What did you mean..."
NEUTRAL ORIENTATION	A	5. ACCEPTS OR USES IDEAS WITHOUT REFERENCE TO SOURCE: Clarifying, building, or developing ideas of others without crediting them with the original thought. (If a person is referred to, it falls into category 2.) E.g. "When I experienced that..." or "You should have seen us when that same thing happened..."
	NT	6. GUIDES DISCUSSION TOWARD CONTENT: Intent is to control topic or flow of discussion. Includes calling back to the subject, a content orientation, and didactic techniques.
	C	7. CRITICIZING: Statements intended to change another's behavior from non-acceptable to acceptable. Criticizing someone. E.g. "You shouldn't..." or "You're wrong."
SELF ORIENTATION	A	8. JUSTIFYING AUTHORITY: Justifying own behavior or ideas by an outside source. E.g. "The Bible says..." or "I read..."
	NT	9. EXPRESSING OWN IDEAS: Giving own facts or opinions. Self-oriented stories and ideas. Mild self-reference.
	C&A	9+ PERSONAL SHARING: Sharing very personal problems not ordinarily discussed outside the family.
		0. SILENCE OR CONFUSION: Communication can't be understood or is non-existent.

*In second column above: C.means concern; A.means acceptance;
NT. means non-threatening.

Note. From William L. Bass, A Project in Leadership Development For a Local Church's Ministry of Evangelism Through Small Group Interaction, 1977. Reprinted by permission.

e.g. category 3 is "Other Person Oriented" in that it relieves tension in the group through levity, but it is neutral because it takes the edge off of other forms of interaction. In the same way category 6 is neutral because of a content orientation. Category 9 has a "Self Orientation" because of the ownership of the subject matter, but it is neutral in that it does not promote further interaction.

Category 9+ is a special category. It is most definitely "Self Oriented," but is the kind of inter-action which builds bridges to an "Other Person Orientation." It is a sharing category of a deeply personal and meaningful nature, and therefore reflects a concern and acceptance of self primarily, but also a concern and acceptance of others by the fact that the sharing is taking place.

Through the use of these categories in coding the interaction of the thirteen sessions of the study group, I can determine the process of the group in the three basic orientations, or the eleven categories, as well as of individual members in the group through an objective measurable system.

One last comment about this interaction analysis: in most systems of interaction analysis a check and balance system is employed by having more than one observer, and by calculating a reliability factor. This I did not do for three reasons: first, I did not have another trained observer available; second, I feared intimidating the members of the small group with too many observers; and third, the reliability of one observer was in my estimation enough for the purposes of evaluating this project.

* * * * * * * * * * * * * * * * * *

Table 8-2 shows a summary of the interaction analysis data from group session 9. It shows that group member "A" was clearly the leader. "A" was the only person to "guide discussion toward content" (category 6). Group member "D" tended more than others to express his or her own ideas and to share (categories 9 and 9+). The "participation frequency distribution" shows that the group was leader dominated, and that there was little silence or confusion. For the most part, the focus of the group was on expressing individual ideas.

153

If your concern is with small group functioning, such data can be useful.

Table 8-2

Example of Analysis of Interaction Data

SESSION 9

MEMBERS	1	2	3	4	5	6	7	8	9	9+	TOTALS
A	20	55	0	48	0	839	0	0	269	67	1,298
B	0	24	0	12	0	0	0	22	186	1	245
C	0	13	3	10	0	0	0	4	85	0	115
D	0	11	0	28	2	0	0	0	284	24	349
E	0	1	0	0	1	0	0	0	46	0	48
F	--	--	--	--	--	--	--	--	--	--	--
G	0	13	0	30	8	0	0	7	253	0	311
TOTALS	20	117	3	128	11	839	0	33	1,123	92	2,366

Category 0 -- 69   Total Coding Units -- 2,435

Participation Frequency Distribution			Category Frequency Distribution		
Member	f	%	Category	f	%
A --	1,298 --	53.31	9 --	1,123 --	46.12
D --	349 --	14.33	6 --	839 --	34.46
G --	311 --	12.77	4 --	128 --	5.26
B --	245 --	10.06	2 --	117 --	4.80
C --	115 --	4.72	9+ --	92 --	3.78
#0 --	69 --	2.83	0 --	69 --	2.83
E --	48 --	1.97	8 --	33 --	1.36
			1 --	20 --	0.82
			5 --	11 --	0.45
			3 --	3 --	0.12
			7 --	0 --	0.00

CHAPTER IX

HOW TO TALK LIKE AN EXPERT:
BASIC STATISTICAL CONCEPTS

Statistical analysis is a field that few clergy
have studied. That's the reason for this chapter.
The field is complex and subtle enough that one chapter will not meet all of your needs as you design your
study and analyze your data. You will want to refer
to an introductory statistics textbook, and may want to
consult an expert, but this chapter should help you
use these resources intelligently.

The study of New Testament Greek provides a good
comparison to the study of statistical analysis. A
person can develop a basic utilitarian knowledge of
Greek fairly easily. That is, a person can easily
learn to transliterate and prounounce Greek words,
learn a basic vocabulary, have an elementary conceptual understanding of the tenses, and learn to use a
lexicon. This level of knowledge is usually sufficient for a person to make intelligent use of academic
commentaries, such as volumes in the International
Critical Commentary series.

Beyond this beginning level, the study of Greek
becomes quite complicated, and scholars have heated
arguments about certain technical problems.

In statistical analysis, it is not difficult to
develop a conceptual understanding of basic tools such
as "probability," "mean," "standard deviation,"
"significant difference," and "correlation." You can
also easily learn to understand the meaning of the
basic mathematical formulas and compute standard
deviations and correlations. Such computations are
tedious, but not difficult. They require nothing more
than elementary school arithmetic. Given an elementary
knowledge of statistical analysis, you can begin to
read intelligently articles in publications such as
the Journal for the Scientific Study of Religion.

Following the analogy with Greek, beyond the
elementary level, complications and subtleties abound.
If your particular project happens to require a statistical tool which is subject to controversy, trust

the consultation of an expert, just as you would if,
in sermon preparation, you came across an exegetical
problem beyond your understanding.

How to Approach Statistics

For many people, the word "statistics" is
loaded with emotional baggage, and the emotions are
usually negative. Then most common responses to the
word are "boring" or "frightening." The "boring"
response comes from a mental association of "statistics"
with incomprehensible tables of numbers. The "frightening" response comes from a widespread discomfort with
mathematics, and thus with the process of statistical
analysis.

In addition, people are concerned that statistics
can be easily manipulated to obscure the truth.
Disraeli has been quoted as saying, "There are three
kinds of lies: lies, damned lies and statistics."
The problem that concerned Disraeli is partly the
result of a wide-spread lack of understanding of statistics and partly the result of conscious falsification
on the part of some poeple (particularly in advertis-
ing) who report statistical data. Both Huff (1954) and
Campbell (1974) have written entertaining and authori-
tative books intended to help the reader read statistical reports with discernment. You will benefit from
reading either or both of these works.

In recent years, people in many fields of academic study have found statistical analysis useful. Even
historians have been analyzing quantitative data.
Consequently, statistics courses have been taught in
many different university departments, and there has
been a proliferation of statistics texts. This is to
the student's benefit.

I have never found an introductory statistics
textbook that I could recommend without reservation,
but almost all statistics textbooks I have examined
include at least one chapter that seemed to me to be
clearly written and enlightening. My basic suggestion,
therefore, is that once you have determined what statistical tool you need, go to a university library and
sit down with the shelf of statistics textbooks.
Select several that include a chapter that deals with
your problem. One of these will probably tell you what
you need to know in language you will understand.

All of these books will include equations that look strange, but the examples worked out in this chapter should help you puzzle through the textbook equations. If you find an equation that seems important, but you do not understand it, ask someone in a university department of psychology, sociology or education to explain it.

How do you determine what statistical tool you need? First phrase your question as clearly and concisely as possible, preferably in one sentence. Identify the variables and their values. Then ask someone who knows something about statistical analysis, perhaps a fellow student, perhaps a business person in your congregation, perhaps a professor of research methodology.

Statistical Concepts and Definitions

The purpose of this section is to give you a general understanding of the concepts that will be most useful to you. These are not precise definitions. We will say more about some of these concepts later in the chapter.

Mean. Given a list of numbers, you compute the mean by adding the numbers and dividing by the number of numbers. This is the "average" you learned to compute in grade school.

Median. This is another kind of "average." Given a list of numbers arranged from highest to lowest, the median is the number in the middle. If you have an even number of numbers, the median is the mean of the two middle numbers (add the two middle numbers and divide by two).

Mode. A third kind of "average." Given a list of numbers, the mode is that number which appears most frequently.

Range. Given a list of numbers, the highest and lowest numbers indicate the range.

Normal distribution. Given a list of numbers arranged from highest to lowest, they will be "normally distributed" if they meet certain mathematical criteria. These criteria need not concern us, but we will be interested in certain properties of the normal distribution. Among other things, the normal distribution is symmetrical about the mean. The mean, median and mode are identical in the normal distribution. Approximately 68% of the numbers will lie within one standard deviation (see below) either side of the mean.

Standard deviation. This is a number which can be calculated from your list of numbers and the number of numbers in your list. If your numbers are approximately normally distributed, the standard deviation gives a quick estimate of how "spread out" the numbers are. If you know the mean, range and standard deviation of a list of numbers, you can form a pretty good mental picture of the list. Given two lists of numbers, the mean and standard deviation are essential if you want to compare them.

Correlation. A comparison of two sets of numbers is a correlation. By far the most common measure of correlation is the "Pearson product-moment correlation coefficient," commonly called "Pearson's r." Calculating Pearson's r will give you a number between "+1" and "-1." If everyone who scores well on one test scores well on a second test, and vice-versa, the correlation will be close to "+1." If everyone who scores well on the first test scores poorly on the second test, and vice versa, the correlation will be close to "-1." A random relation between scores on the two tests will produce a "0" correlation. We will say much more below.

Significant difference. Measure anything twice, and you will get at least a slight variation in measurements. Thus, if you ask people to complete a questionnaire on commitment to the church before and after confirmation class, the mean score for the class will probably not be identical before and after. How do we compare the two mean scores? The difference is statistically significant if a similar difference would appear if the project were to be re-done an infinite number of times. Note that the concept of statistical significance has to do only with the stability of a difference, not its magnitude. It is not unusual to find a difference which is statistically significant, but of little practical importance. Statistical calculations can determine whether or not a difference is (likely to be) significant.

Level of significance. If a difference between two means is statistically significant, how many times will the same difference be found if the project is

158

repeated 100 times? If the difference will be found 95 out of 100 times, we say the difference is significant at the 95% level, and in writing it is commonly noted as p < .05 (the probability of their being the same is less than 5%). Level of significance is frequently calculated by what are called chi-square tests, t-tests or F-tests. In journal articles you may see them reported something like this: t = 1.729, p < .05.

Analysis of variance. A statistical tool for looking for significant differences among several groups of people on a test or other measures. Sometimes abbreviated ANOVA. It is complicated because the procedure for doing the arithmetical calculations changes when the "design" of the experiment changes. It is particularly useful if you want to test the effectiveness of various combinations of treatments (such as when testing drugs or teaching students). In the church, we seldom subject people to systematic variations in treatments, so ANOVA will probably not be an appropriate tool for very many D. Min. projects.

One Basic Distinction: Two Kinds of Analysis

There are two basic kinds of statistical analysis: descriptive and inferential.

Inferential statistical analysis is a tool for predicting the future based on past observations. Inferential questions are not always stated in terms of prediction, but a little thought shows that prediction is implied in them.

For example, a question such as, "Will adults learn more about praying and observing a devotional life from (a) a course based on contemporary devotional books, or (b) a course based on classic devotional books?" implies a prediction. If the research study shows that (b) is more effective than (a), the prediction is that you would lead a more effective course in the future if you concentrated on classic books. This is a simple (and not very realistic) question that would (probably) involve a simple tool of inferential analysis, one-way analysis of variance.

Descriptive analysis is concerned with the data at hand. We cannot comprehend a page full of numbers, so we use descriptive tools in an attempt to summarize them. For example, computing an average (any kind of

average) will give us one number that in some sense
describes the entire page of numbers.

This chapter is primarily concerned with descriptive tools. One reason for this is that the descriptive tools are useful for a broad range of problems
likely to be addressed in D. Min. theses. A second
reason is that the use of inferential techniques is
far too complex a subject to be discussed in this book.
Analysis of variance, for example, assumes as many
forms as a Greek verb. The set-up for ANOVA may depend
on the number of variables, the number of cases, how
many times your people take a test, and other things.

Another Basic Distinction: Levels of Measurement

Statisticians speak of four levels of measurement: "nominal," "ordinal," "interval," and "ratio."
Only the first three are of interest to us, because
we will never encounter ratio data in our obeservations
of people and society.

Why is this categorization of data important?
As a "rule of thumb," it is valid to use any tool of
statistical analysis with ratio data. A more select
set of statistical tools may be used validly with
interval data, including those that are used with
nominal and ordinal data. A smaller set of tools may
be used with ordinal data, and a still smaller set with
nominal data. In other words, the categories of
measurement are "nested" (Figure 9-1).

Interval measurement is characterized by an
ordering of categories such that each category width
is equal. A common ruler measures in intervals. If a
pencil is two inches long and another pencil is three
inches long, we know the first one is two-thirds the
length of the second.

An ordinal measure divides the property being
measured into categories such that it is valid to
designate the categories as "first," "second," "third,"
and such, but we cannot assume equal category widths.
Many questionnaires provide ordinal measures.

Consider this item from a religiosity survey:
"How often do you talk about religion with your friends,
neighbors, or fellow workers?" You are to choose one
of four answers: "regularly," "occasionally,"

"seldom," or "never." Let us assign these four answers scores of 3, 2, 1, and 0, respectively. This will be a perfectly satisfactory ordinal measurement, but it is certainly not interval. You cannot reasonably argue that a person who talks about religion "occasionally" (score, 2) is two-thirds as religious as a person who talks about religion "regularly" (score, 3).

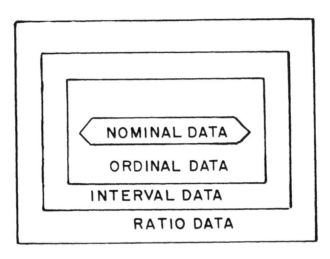

Figure 9-1. Relation among statistical analysis techniques appropriate for various measurement levels.

You cannot compute a meaningful "mean" (arithmetic average) score from ordinal data, while calculation of a mean score is usually the first thing to do in analyzing interval data. Suppose you want to see how often members of a Sunday school class talk about religion, so you ask them the religiosity survey question. Two people say, "regularly," five say, "occasionally," four say, "seldom" and four say, "never." The mean score is one and one-third, which seems to be more than "seldom," and less than "occasionally," but what does it really mean? We cannot say, because we do not know how wide each of the categories is. "Occasionally" is probably a much wider category than the others.

The gradations in increasing understanding of theological concepts do not lend themselves to "right" vs. "wrong" answers and interval scaling. That is why Privette's "Concept Evaluation Test" (appendix) is an

161

ordinal test. For example, consider the question,
"What is God's grace?" The choices, from worst to
best are:

1. God's grace is to say a prayer to God before
   you eat.
2. God shed his grace on thee.
3. God's grace is the kind things God does for
   us.
4. God's grace is God's love and understanding
   for us.
5. God's grace is God's unfailing forgiveness
   and mercy.
6. God's grace is the free gift of God which is
   given to us because of God's love.

Evidently response #6 is "better" than response #5,
and response #3 is "better" than response #2. However,
it is not clear that the same "distance" of "better"
lies between 6 and 5 as between 3 and 2.

As the name implies, data are nominal if they
name categories without regard to order or quantity.
If you are studying the churches of your county, you
may assign them identification numbers. If these
numbers are unrelated to any other variable, they
are nominal. The numbers worn by members of a basket-
ball team are nominal. Sex, eye color and clinical
diagnoses are nominal.

In practice, it is not always easy to distinguish
between interval and ordinal data or between ordinal
and nominal data. For example, the Likert scale
(strongly agree = 4, agree = 3, undecided = 2, disagree
= 1, strongly disagree = 0) is certainly ordinal, but
is it an interval measure? Strictly speaking, maybe
not, but it comes close enough that it is usually
(and appropriately) treated as providing interval
data.

When you design tests and questionnaires, it is
to your advantage if they can provide you with interval data, because you will have a wide variety of
tools available for statistical analysis. If you
cannot design them to provide interval data, you
should be aware of that fact, so you do not use invalid techniques of analysis that lead to unsupport-
able conclusions.

162

For example, consider a study by Embree (1973).
His aim was to offer evidence that a test he devised,
called the Religious Association Scale (RAS) actually
measured "religiousness." He asked people to complete
the RAS, and he also asked them to answer several
questions. Then he used the descriptive statistical
techniques of correlation and factor analysis to see
how responses on RAS related to the other questions.

One of the questions Embree asked was, "Check
the one religious viewpoint that best describes you."
(Conservative, Liberal, Non-religious). Do you see
the trap into which Embree has fallen? This is a
nominal measure. There is no valid way to correlate
nominal data, and factor analysis depends on correlation. All of the correlations with this item are
meaningless, and Embree's factor analysis is consequently thrown off.

How can we analyze nominal data? Rummel (1970,
p. 257) suggests that each option in a question such
as Embree's be treated as a separate "yes-no"
(dichotomous) question. For each respondent, record
a score for "conservative" (yes = 1, no = 2),
"liberal" (yes = 1, no = 2), and "not-religious"
(yes = 1, no = 2). Embree should then have used the
"rank biseral" and "point biseral" correlation techniques to calculate the relationship between each of
these three scores and any of the other scores that
concern him. (The correlation between any two of the
three responses to the question would be measured by
a phi coefficient, but this need not be calculated,
because their correlation will be zero.) These
correlation techniques are specialized and not used
frequently. For a discussion of them, see Glass and
Stanley (1970, pp. 158-181).

Over the years, there has been a great deal of
academic discussion about levels of measurement. If
you are interested in following the arguments, see
bibliographies in Glass and Stanley (1970, pp. 12-13)
and Rummel (1970, p. 221, footnote).

How to Read and Use a Basic Formula:
Standard Deviation

If you want to describe responses of a group to
a questionnaire item or some other data set, reporting
the mean is a good place to begin, but the mean by

163

itself is not enough. Consider the hypothetical case
in Table 9-1. It shows typical Sunday morning worship
attendance at five churches in each of two towns.

Table 9-1

Hypothetical Worship Attendance Data

| CHURCH | TOWN | |
	A	B
1	125	300
2	125	95
3	125	55
4	125	50
5	50	50
Total	550	550
Mean	110	110
Median	125	55
Mode	125	50
Standard Deviation	34	107.9

In each case, the mean is 110, but clearly the cases
are quite different. The description is improved if
you report the range in each case (town "A," 50 to 125,
town "B," 50 to 300), and you can also report the
median and mode for each town to improve your description of the data set.

Another useful and widely used tool for describing a set of data is the standard deviation. The larger
the standard deviation, the more "spread out" the numbers in the data set. A report of the mean, range and
standard deviation gives a concise and useful summary
of most data for most purposes. (As we shall see, if
the data set is "normally distributed," the standard
deviation gives the range for practical purposes.)

Since the standard deviation is both important
and easy to calculate, it can provide a good demonstration of statistical notation. One version of the formula is:

$$\text{standard deviation} = \sqrt{\frac{\sum_{i=1}^{n} (X_i - \bar{X})^2}{n-1}}$$

164

where n is the number of elements in the data set, and X_i represents each of the numbers in the data set. $\overline{X}$ represents the mean of the data set. The upper case sigma ($\sum$) is a symbol for addition, and $\sum\limits_{i=1}^{n}$ means sum all of the expressions containing X_i, from 1 to n. As you probably recall from a long ago math course, the superscript "2" means square what is inside the parentheses. Once you complete the entire calculation, take the square root. Table 9-2, calulation of the standard deviation for the Table 9-1 data from town "B," should make the calculation process clear.

Table 9-2

Demonstration of Standard Deviation Calculation

Xi	(Xi - $\overline{X}$)	(Xi - $\overline{X}$)^2
X_1 = 300	300 - 110 = 190	190 x 190 = 36,100
X_2 = 95	95 - 110 = -15	(-15) x (-15) = 225
X_3 = 55	55 - 110 = -55	(-55) x (-55) = 3,025
X_4 = 50	50 - 110 = -60	(-60) x (-60) = 3,600
X_5 = 50	50 - 110 = -60	(-60) x (-60) = 3,600
		Sum = 46,550

$$\text{Standard Deviation} = \sqrt{\frac{46,550}{4}} = \sqrt{11,637.5} = 107.9$$

If you are working with a large data file, you may want to look into the possibility of using a computer to do the caldulations. If you find yourself using factor analysis (see chapter 6) or some other analysis that requires many calculations, you will probably want to contract with a university computer center. It is fairly easy to calculate standard deviations, correlations and similar analyses on a microcomputer if you have a data processing package.

Standard Deviation and Normal Distribution

Most large data sets that you might work with will be approximately normally distributed. (The data in Table 9-1 are definitely not normally distributed.) Given normally distributed data, the descriptive power of the standard deviation is at its peak, because in any normal distribution, approximately:

1. 68% of the data will be within one standard deviation of the mean either way (34% above the mean, 34% below the mean).
2. 95% of the data will be within two standard deviations of the mean either way.
3. 99.7% of the data will be within three standard deviations of the mean either way.

Figure 9-2 is a familiar graphic representation of a normal distribution which can be found in many textbooks.

As an example, if the mean height of a group of people is 67.5 inches and the standard deviation is 3 inches, 68% of the people will be between 62.5 inches and 70.5 inches tall. Almost no one will be shorter than 58.5 inches or taller than 76.5 inches (three standard deviations either side of the mean).

A "real life" example is drawn from Whelan and Adler (1982). They surveyed directors of religious education in Catholic churches in the Chicago area to (among other things) find out how happy they were in their job. Somewhat to their surprise, they found the job satisfaction data approximated a normal curve (Figure 9-3). In discussing this they said,

> Probably the most important discovery was that DRE's are not as unhappy with their priests as was originally thought. The answers reflected a normal curve. Out of a possible score of 300, which would have meant perfect happiness, there was an average score of 185, with 66% of the respondents falling between the scores of 154 and 217. This curve, instead of being normal, could have been very high on the unhappy side. It was not.

Even when one takes the response
set bias into consideration, and indeed
this is a valid critique, the fact still
remains that the majority of DRE's did
answer the survey more positively than
was predicted. If people were as unhappy
as was thought, and as they seemed to be
saying, it seems likely that this would
have appeared on the survey. There were
places for comments, but only a few were
given. (pp. 3-4)

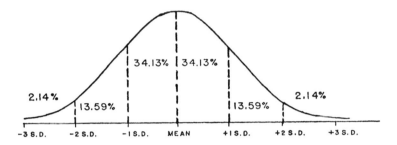

Figure 9-2.   The Normal Curve. Percentages are
percent of cases represented by area
under normal curve.

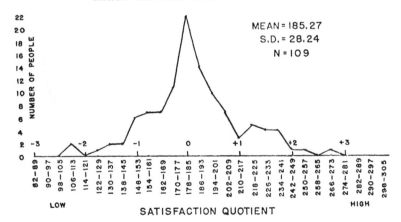

Figure 9-3.   Satisfaction of Chicago Area Directors of
Religious Education with their job.   From
Whelan and Adler, 1982.

167

Correlation

Many of the questions you will want to ask are correlation questions: questions of how one variable is related to another. In this section we will demonstrate two of the most common correlation procedures.

Pearson Product-Moment Correlation Coefficient

The Pearson Product-Moment Correlation Coefficient, commonly called "Pearson's $\underline{r}$" can be calculated with the following formula:

$$\underline{r} = \frac{n \sum x_i y_i - (\sum x_i)(\sum y_i)}{\sqrt{[n \sum x_i^2 - (\sum x_i)^2][n \sum y_i^2 - (\sum y_i)^2]}}$$

The formula is not as difficult as it may seem at first glance. Once again, $\underline{n}$ is the number of cases. The X's are one variable, and the Y's are the other variable. On the sigmas, we have omitted the specification that you should add from 1 to n, because it is obvious that that is what is to be done. As you can see, to calculate a correlation, you need paired observations. If you are distributing a questionnaire before and after teaching a class, you will need to be able to match each person's "before" and "after" responses.

A couple of subtleties are worth noting. First, $\sum x^2$, which means square each X and then add the squares, is not the same as $(\sum x)^2$, which means add the X's and then square the sum. Second, if you are working with a pocket calculater, in the denominator you will probably be trying to take the square root of a number larger than your calculator will handle. If so, take the square root of each term in the product. "The square root of a product equals the product of the square roots."

The procedure is demonstrated in Table 9-3, using data from Corbett (1979). He had taught a six session Sunday school class to some children, and reported the number of classes they attended and the number of correct answers on a final test. The question we are asking (not his question, but ours) is whether there is a tendency for those who attended

168

Table 9-3

Demonstration of Correlation Calculation

PUPIL NUMBER	SESSIONS ATTENDED(X)	X^2	SCORE(Y)	Y^2	XY
1	2	4	18	324	36
2	3	9	18	324	54
3	1	1	23	529	23
4	4	16	25	625	100
5	3	9	25	625	75
6	4	16	20	400	80
7	5	25	28	784	140
8	0	0	16	256	0
9	1	1	25	625	25
10	2	4	20	400	40
11	3	9	21	441	63
12	3	9	15	225	45
13	3	9	24	576	72
14	1	1	19	361	19
15	2	4	27	729	54
16	5	25	20	400	100
17	3	9	24	576	72
18	0	0	23	529	0
19	5	25	13	169	65
20	5	25	16	256	80
21	5	25	18	324	90
22	6	36	28	784	168
	66	262	466	10,262	1,401

$$r = \frac{22\,(1401) - (66)\,(466)}{\sqrt{[(22)(262) - (66)(66)]\,[(22)(10,262) - (466)(466)]}}$$

$$r = \frac{30,822 - 30,756}{\sqrt{(5764 - 4356)\,(225,764 - 217,156)}}$$

$$r = \frac{66}{\sqrt{(1408)(8608)}} = \frac{66}{\sqrt{1408}\sqrt{8608}}$$

$$r = \frac{66}{(37.5)(92.7)} = \frac{66}{3479.2} = .019$$

Note. Data from Warren G. Corbett, (1979).

169

the most sessions to get the highest score. The
calculation is presented in Table 9-3.

The correlation, r = .019, indicates that there
is no linear relationship between attendance at
Corbett's class and test scores at the end of the
course. Figure 9-4 is a graphic demonstration of this
lack of relationship. It is a scattergram with the
number of classes attended indicated on the horizontal axis (also called the abscissa or x-axis), and the
final test score on the vertical axis (or ordinate or
y-axis). For r = 1, or r = -1, the scattergram would
be a straight line.

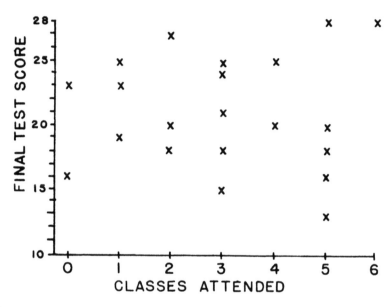

Figure 9-4.   Scattergram of Corbett's (1979) Data and
              classes attended and score on final test.

Sometimes (not too often), the scattergram will
be a curved line, which is a definite relationship,
even though it is not linear. In such a case, the
value of r (a test for linear relationship) will be low.
If you suspect a curved relationship, check for it by
plotting a scattergram.

Ordinal Data Correlation

Pearson's r is a tool for analyzing interval data. It can be applied to ordinal data (and when it is, is named the Spearman Rank Correlation Coefficient). Another, perhaps simpler ordinal correlation tool is Kendall's tau.

For example, in a study of opinion on how the pastor's time should be used, the pastor-parish relations committee ranked 12 tasks, and the pastor ranked the same 12 tasks (Table 9-4, data from Snider, 1976). This is certainly ordinal data.

The formula for calculating Kendall's tau is:

$$\Upsilon = \frac{P - Q}{\sqrt{[n(n - 1)/2]} - T_x \quad \sqrt{[n(n-1)/2]} - T_y}$$

where T_x and T_y are corrections for tied ranks. If there are no tied ranks, T_x and T_y are zero, and the formula simplifies to:

$$\Upsilon = \frac{P - Q}{n(n - 1)/2}$$

where n is the number of sources of rankings. In Table 9-4, n refers to the 12 ways the pastor might use time.

P is the total number of "agreements," and Q is the total number of "inversions." To find P and Q, arrange one of the rankings in its natural order (1, 2, 3, etc.). Call that ranking X, and the other one Y. Take the top rank on X ("preaching and worship" in Table 9-4), and count the number of Y ranks below it that are larger. This is your number of "agreements." The number of Y ranks below it that are smaller is the number of "inversions." Do the same for each item in turn. The technique is difficult to explain discursively, but not difficult to do. Practice it on Table 9-4. If you have questions, consult almost any statistics text (cf. Siegel, 1956, pp. 213-219).

171

Table 9-4

Demonstration of Kendall's Tau Calculation

TASK	X = COMMITTEE RANK	Y = PASTOR RANK	AGREEMENTS	INVERSIONS
Preaching & Worship	1	2	10	1
Evangelism	2	7	5	5
Leader Among Leaders	3.5	1	9	0
Personal & Spiritual Growth	3.5	5	6	2
Visiting	5	3	7	0
Administration	6	6	5	1
Counseling	7	4	5	0
THE Leader	8	10.5	0	1
Teaching	9	8	3	0
Community Leader	10	10.5	0	0
Denominational Responsibilities	11	10.5	0	0
Enabler	12	10.5	0	0
			P = 50	Q = 10

$$T_x = \tfrac{1}{2}\sum t(t - 1) = \tfrac{1}{2}(2)(2 - 1) = 1$$

$$T_y = \tfrac{1}{2}\sum t(t - 1) = \tfrac{1}{2}[4(4 - 1)] = \tfrac{1}{2}(12) = 6$$

$$\tau = \frac{P - Q}{\sqrt{[n(n-1)/2] - T_x}\ \sqrt{[n(n - 1)/2] - T_y}}$$

$$= \frac{50 - 10}{\sqrt{[12(12 - 1)/2]-1}\ \sqrt{[12(12 - 1)/2]-6}}$$

$$= \frac{40}{\sqrt{65}\ \sqrt{63}} = \frac{40}{(8.06)\,7.94)} = \frac{40}{63.99} = .625$$

Note. Data from Snider, 1976.

172

To find T_x, look at the X column. How many times do you find ties? (One time in Table 9-4.) In each case, how many items are tied? (Two in Table 9-4.) For each case, multiply the number of items tied by that number minus 1. Add all of the cases, and divide the sum by 2. Expressed as a formula it is:

$$T_x = \tfrac{1}{2} \sum t(t-1)$$

where t is the number of items tied in each case of a tie.

The same formula is used to find T_y, examining the Y column. In table 9-4, there is one case, with four tied items.

The example illustrated in Table 9-4 shows a correlation of γ = .625. This is a fairly high correlation. You can get a notion of its practical meaning by examining the table. The outstanding instance of disagreement between the pastor and his committee has to do with the task of evangelism. This disagreement is so sharp that it lowered the correlation quite a bit from what it might otherwise have been.

More than Two Columns of Ordinal Data

Correlation is a measure of relationship between two measurements. Suppose you want to test the degree of agreement among several members of a committee. If they provide you with ordinal data, such as priority ratings, Kendall's Coefficient of Concordance is an easily calculated measure of agreement (Siegel, 1956, 229-238).

The Meaning of Correlation

Goodwin Watson, writing in 1931, illustrated the meaning of various correlation levels this way (pp. 163-164):

.00 is about the relationship between the length of a man's nose and his intelligence. There is no relation at all.

.20 is about the relationship between wealth and intelligence, a very slight tendency for those who have more of one to have more of the other, but great numbers of exceptions.

173

.40 is about the relationship between scores on an intelligence test and college marks earned by juniors and seniors.

.60 is about the relationship between height and weight. Roughly they go together, but there are enough short and heavy, tall and light, to keep the correlation from being very large.

.80 is about the relationship between score on one form of a long standard objective test of reading ability, and on another form of the same test taken a few hours later. Generally the agreement between the two is good.

.99 is about the relationship between the weights of a series of small objects weighed on a good scale by a competent person, and the same series weighed again, a few moments later, on the same scale by the same person.

Then he offered "a few results obtained from studies of significance for religious education arranged in order of the size of the reported correlation." (p.164)

.82 Group having high information score about Japan and group being favorably disposed toward Japanese, wishing liberal policies of our government toward them.

.73 Honesty of child and honesty of his best friend in the same class.

.55 Delinquency and defective home discipline.

.48 Satisfaction with one's religion and general happiness in life.

.44 Religious home training and amount of church participation in college.

.39 Age of boy and age of chum.

.36 Intelligence and radical ideas in religion.

.33 Honesty of child and honesty of big brother or sister.

.30 Freedom from race prejudice and number of friends among foreign students.

.28 Sense of guilt in childhood, adolescence, and adult shyness, self-consciousness.

174

.26 Dullness (low I.Q.) and per cent of times child attempted deception in a series of tests.

.22 Religious home training and self-described as morbidly conscientious.

.19 Group being well informed on Orient and unfavorable toward missionary enterprises.

.18 Freedom from race prejudice and intelligence.

.15 Delinquency and poverty in the home.

.13 Intelligence and dissatisfaction with one's religion.

.01 Biblical information and willingness to cooperate loyally for group.

.00 Biblical information and honesty in school tests.

Incidentally, there have been a fiarly large number of studies of Biblical knowledge and behavior (mostly Master's and Doctoral theses), uniformly finding little relationship. Several years ago the author reviewed most of these studies, and observed that the tests of Biblical knowledge seldom included any questions about the teachings of the Old Testament prophets or other ethical teachings in the scripture. This is a major deficiency in the existing research which has not yet been remedied. Methodologically speaking, the best such study the present author has reviewed was a 1948 Ph.D. dissertation by Robert Edward Harlow at the University of Toronto, Bible Knowledge and Ideals of Verbal Honesty.

When are Two Numbers Different?

Any time you measure something twice, you will probably obtain two different results, no matter how slight the difference. If the difference is large, you measure again, because you must have made a mistake one of the times. If the difference is small, you attribute it to measurement error and ignore it.

Similarly, you may measure what you think are two different things, such as attitudes before and after participation in some experience. The results will not be exactly the same, but are they really different? If the difference is small, they are

175

probably not different. The results are due to measurement error, and attitudes did not change.

A minimal criterion for difference is found in statistical significance. A difference between two mean scores is said to be "statistically significant" if its predictable stability is high. A widely used standard is that a difference is statistically significant if the difference will be at least that large in 95 out of 100 independent measurements. (The notion of the difference being "at least that large" is not the definition of statistical significance, but is a practical consequence of that definition.)

For example, in a study of teenagers, Baptist males from the south had a mean score of 9.56 on a "religious practice" survey (including items such as frequency of church attendance). Baptist females from the south had a mean score of 11.04 on the same survey (Nelsen & Potvin, 1981, Table 3). Is this 1.48 point difference significant? Yes. The authors report that a difference that large will occur by change only one time in 100 independent observations. In other words, the difference is stable.

In statistical notation, this 1.48 point difference is noted as $p < .01$. "p" stands for probability. " $<$ " is standard mathematical notation for "less than" ("$>$" means "greater than"). The notation means that there is a 1% probability that the 1.48 point difference was due to chance.

Is the 1.48 point difference important? That is a quite different question, and in this case we do not have enough information to answer it. A statistically significant difference does not have to be large enough to be important. Furthermore, the larger the sample, the smaller the difference required for statistical significance. The Nelson and Potvin study employed a fairly large sample, so read closely before asserting that Southern Baptist girls are more religious than Southern Baptist boys. Before making that judgement, you would have to examine the survey form and see how it is scored.

In summary, a difference between means will not be important unless it is statistically significant (the usual standard being $p < .05$), but a difference between means can be statistically significant and still be unimportant.

176

Student's t Test: A Test of Differences

One of the most commonly used statistical tools for determining whether or not two mean scores are statistically different is the t-test. It is sometimes called "Student's t," because the author who developed the test published it under the pseudonym, "A Student."

If your samples are independent of each other, the formula for the t-test is:

$$t = \frac{M_1 - M_2}{\sqrt{\left(\frac{\sum d_1{}^2 + \sum d_2{}^2}{n_1 + n_2 - 2}\right)\left(\frac{1}{n_1} + \frac{1}{n_2}\right)}}$$

where M_1 is the mean of the first sample,

M_2 is the mean of the second sample,

d_1 is the deviation from the mean of the first sample,

d_2 is the deviation from the mean of the second sample,

n_1 is the number of people in the first sample, and

n_2 is the number of people in the second sample.

Corbett (1979, pp. 86-91) asked Sunday school attenders and non-attenders to respond on a Likert scale ("strongly agree" = 1, "strongly disagree" = 5) to several statements, one of which was, "The Bible is hard to understand." The responses and the set-up for the t-test are in Table 9-5.

The calculation is as follows:

$$t = \frac{2.4 - 2.1}{\sqrt{\left(\frac{19.44 + 20.96}{14 + 16 - 2}\right)\left(\frac{1}{14} + \frac{1}{16}\right)}} = .682$$

Table 9-5

Response to "The Bible is Hard to Understand"

ATTENDERS				NON-ATTENDERS				
No.	MEAN(M_1)	SCORE	DEVIATION	(d_1)	No.	MEAN(M_1)	SCORE	DEVIATION (d_1)
1	2.4	2	.4	.16	1	2.1	2	.1 .01
2	2.4	1	1.4	1.96	2	2.1	3	-.9 .81
3	2.4	2	.4	.16	3	2.1	1	1.1 1.21
4	2.4	1	1.4	1.96	4	2.1	4	-1.9 3.61
5	2.4	4	-1.6	2.56	5	2.1	1	1.1 1.21
6	2.4	3	-.6	.36	6	2.1	1	1.1 1.21
7	2.4	4	-1.6	2.56	7	2.1	4	-1.9 3.61
8	2.4	2	.4	.16	8	2.1	1	1.1 1.21
9	2.4	4	-1.6	2.56	9	2.1	1	1.1 1.21
10	2.4	4	-1.6	2.56	10	2.1	2	.1 .01
11	2.4	1	1.4	1.96	11	2.1	2	.1 .01
12	2.4	3	-.6	.36	12	2.1	3	-.9 .81
13	2.4	2	.4	.16	13	2.1	1	1.1 1.21
14	2.4	1	1.4	1.96	14	2.1	1	1.1 1.21
SUM		34		19.44	15	2.1	2	.1 .01
					16	2.1	4	-1.9 3.61
					SUM		33	20.96

$n_1 = 14$ $n_2 = 16$

$$t = \frac{2.4 - 2.1}{\sqrt{\left(\frac{19.44 + 20.96}{14 + 16 - 2}\right)\left(\frac{1}{14} + \frac{1}{16}\right)}}$$

$$t = \frac{.3}{\sqrt{.19}} = \frac{.3}{.44} = .682$$

Alternate - Eliminate 2 who scored 1.

$$t = \frac{2.4 - 2.2}{\sqrt{\left(\frac{19.44 + 18.36}{14 + 14 - 2}\right)\left(\frac{1}{14} + \frac{1}{14}\right)}}$$

$$t = \frac{.2}{\sqrt{\left(\frac{37.80}{26}\right)\left(\frac{1}{7}\right)}} = \frac{.2}{\sqrt{\frac{1.45}{7}}} = \frac{.2}{.46} = .434$$

Eliminate 2 who scored 4.

$$t = \frac{2.4 - 1.8}{\sqrt{\left(\frac{19.44 + 12.36}{26}\right)\left(\frac{1}{7}\right)}} = \frac{.6}{\sqrt{.175}} = \frac{.6}{.418} = 1.44$$

178

Whether or not the t score is significant depends on the "degrees of freedom." For the t-test, calculate the degrees of freedom as $\underline{d.f.} = n_1 + n_2 - 2$. In this case, $\underline{d.f.} = 28$. A table of t distributions (found in any statistics textbook) shows that there is no significant difference between the means of these two groups. There seems to be no difference between Sunday school attenders and non-attenders in perceived difficulty of understanding the Bible.

For comparison, another of Corbett's items was, "The Bible doesn't make sense to me." Attenders scored: 5, 2, 5, 3, 4, 3, 1, 4, 3, 4, 2, 3, 4 ($\underline{n}$ = 13). Non-attenders scored: 4, 3, 3, 2, 2, 3, 4, 2, 2, 2, 2, 3, 2, 4 ($\underline{n}$ = 14). You may want to calculate the t score as an exercise. t = 1.538, $\underline{d.f.}$ = 25. This does not reach significance at the .05 level.

This is an interesting result. Although both statements say about the same thing, with one being the reverse of the other, the second statement is personalized, and because of social pressure or some other reason, it might have gotten a different response from the attenders than from the non-attenders. That did not happen. On the average, both groups responded the same to both items.

A technical word of caution is appropriate. The t-test is valid only for comparing two groups. Suppose you want to compare test results of three or more Sunday school classes. Do not do repeated comparisons using the t-test. Several alternative statistical tools are available. To choose the right one, talk with a statistical consultant.

If you are testing "matched" (non-independent) samples (such as one sibling or spouse in one group and the second sibling or spouse in the second group), Equation 6 will underestimate the value of t, possibly causing statistically significant differences to be overlooked. For information in the t-test for matched samples, see any introductory statistics textbook.

Chi-Square: An Inferential Tool

Chi-square analysis is a simple and widely used tool for identifying significant differences between or among groups. One nice feature of chi-square analysis is that it can be used with any level of measurement.

Chi-square analysis is useful whenever you can make a reasonable estimate of how groups would relate on a random basis. You can compare the actual data with the expected (random) data, and see if the difference is significant.

A simplified version of the formula is:

$$\chi^2 = \sum \frac{(O - E)^2}{E}$$

where O symbolizes the actual (observed) data, and E symbolizes the expected data.

To take a simple example, Glock and Stark (1965, p. 162, Table 8-4) reported how many Protestants scored "high," "medium," and "none" on an "index of religious experience." The total number of Protestants in the survey was 1875. What would a person expect the distribution to be if Protestantism had nothing to do with "religious experience?" People would probably be evenly distributed among the three categories, with each group including 625 people. Given this expectation, we can lay out the data and do the calculation (Table 9-6).

Having calculated the number, you need to determine the number of "degrees of freedom." In this case, since the total is fixed ($\underline{n}$ = 1875), you can insert any numbers into two of the observed cells, and the third cell will be determined. So there are two degrees of freedom. A chi-square table for two degrees of freedom shows that there is much less than a 1% probability that the observed data would turn out to be the same as the expected data in another sample of in a larger sample. In general, the larger the value of chi-square, the more certain you will be of a difference between your data and random data.

How do you decide what is "expected?" You simply need to think about it, and be prepared to defend your answer. Sometimes you might expect a "normal distribution" in your data, such as if you are studying acceptance of an innovation (see chapter 2). In other cases, you might base your expectation on a second, independent survey.

For example, consider the question, does the religious affiliation of American graduate students reflect the American population? Glock and Stark (1965, p. 269, Table 14-2) give us the data in Table 9-7 (collected in 1957 and 1958).

Table 9-6

Demonstration of Chi-Square Calculation

| | Degree of Religious Experience Among Protestants Surveyed | | | |
	HIGH	MEDIUM	LOW	TOTAL
OBSERVED	1087	525	263	1875
EXPECTED	625	625	625	1875

$$\chi^2 = \frac{(1087 - 625)^2}{625} + \frac{(525 - 625)^2}{625} + \frac{(263 - 625)^2}{625}$$

$$\chi^2 = \frac{(462)^2 + (-100)^2 + (-362)^2}{625}$$

$$\chi^2 = \frac{213,444 + 10,000 + 131,044}{625}$$

$$\chi^2 = \frac{354,488}{625} = 567.18 \qquad p < .005$$

Note. Data from Glock and Stark, 1965.

In this case, if there were no relation between pursuing graduate studies and religious affiliation, we would expect graduate student religious affiliation to be the same as religious affiliation in the general population. But we cannot calculate chi-square directly from Table 9-7, because it is not appropriate to calculate chi-square from percentages.

Glock and Stark tell us that the number of graduate students surveyed was 2,842. Given this number, we can construct Table 9-8. The calculation of chi-square shows there is a statistically significant difference between what was observed (actual graduate students) and what might have been expected (proportion of U.S. population).

Table 9-7

A Comparison Between the Religious Affiliations of
American Graduate Students in the Arts and Sciences
And A Cross-Section of the American Population*

	PROTESTANT	CATHOLIC	JEWISH	OTHER	NONE	TOTAL
GRADUATE STUDENTS	38%	22%	9%	5%	26%	100%
U.S. POPULATION	66%	26%	3%	1%	4%	100%

*Source: United States Bureau of the Census, Current Popula-
tion Reports, series P-20, No.79, February 2, 1958.

Note. Total number of Graduate Students = 2,842.
Note. From Charles Y. Glock and Rodney Stark, Religion and
Society in Tension, 1965, p.269. Data from 1957, 1958.
Copyright 1965 by Rand McNally & Company. Reprinted by per-
mission.

Table 9-8

Calculation of Chi-Square on Data in Table 9-7

	RELIGIOUS AFFILIATION					
	PROTESTANT	CATHOLIC	JEWISH	OTHER	NONE	TOTAL
GRADUATE STUDENTS	1080	625	256	142	739	2,842
U.S. POPULATION	1876	739	85	28	114	2,842

$$\chi^2 = \frac{(1080 - 1876)^2}{1876} + \frac{(625 - 739)^2}{739} + \frac{(256 - 85)^2}{85} + \frac{(142 - 28)^2}{28}$$

$$+ \frac{(739 - 114)^2}{114}$$

$$^2 = 337.75 + 17.59 + 344 + 464.14 + 3426.54$$

$$^2 = 4590 \quad \underline{df} = 4 \quad p < .005$$

182

Another type of problem to which chi-square analysis is applicable is testing for the relationship of variables in a "contingency table." A "contingency table" is a chart in which all values of all variables are arrayed so as to allow for all possible combinations of values. Figure 5-1, in the discussion of Paul Tillich, is an example of a contingency table consisting of two variables, one with two values and one with three values.

If each person in your sample can be categorized in one and only one cell of a contingency table, you can use chi-square analysis on the data to see whether or not the two variables are independent.

For example, Fortney (1973) did a study in which the results were presented in a large number of contingency tables. One of his tables categorized seminary students according to whether their mother was Christian or non-Christian, and according to which of five views of God's discipline the seminary students held (Table 9-9).

Table 9-9

Observed and Expected Figures in a Contingency Table
(Mother's Spiritual Status Related To Child's
View of God's Discipline.)

MOTHER'S SPIRITUAL STATUS	GOD'S DISCIPLINE					
	INSUFFICIENT	FIRM, BUT SOMETIMES HARSH OR INCONSISTENT	FIRM, BUT LOVING	HARSH AT TIMES	ADEQUATE BASED ON RESPECT	TOTAL OBSERVED
CHRISTIAN (OBSERVED)	5	1	16	0	2	24
CHRISTIAN (EXPECTED)	4.4	.6	12	2.5	4.4	—
NON-CHRISTIAN (OBSERVED)	2	0	3	4	5	14
NON-CHRISTIAN (EXPECTED)	2.6	.4	7	1.5	2.6	—
TOTAL OBSERVED	7	1	19	4	7	38

Note. Based on data from William Boyd Fortney, 1973.

In Table 9-9, rows 1 and 3 are from Fortney.
Row 5 is the sum of rows 1 and 3. The question we ask
about the data in rows 1 and 3 is, for each view of
God's discipline, does the same proportion of seminary
students with Christian mothers hold that view as the
proportion of seminary students with non-Christian
mothers? If not, then we can infer that the two
variables are related, and we will probably assume
that the status of the mother's faith "caused" the
student's view of God's discipline, rather than the
other way around. (Note that we cannot check the
relation between the two variables with correlation
analysis, because both variables are nominal.)

To find the "expected" values necessary for chi-
square calculation, multiply the row total for each
cell times the column total for that cell, and divide
the product by the grand total of observations. For
example, consider the upper left cell in Table 9-9
(Christian mother, God's discipline insufficient). The
expected value for that cell is:

$$\frac{24 \times 7}{38} = \frac{168}{38} = 4.421.$$

You may want to calculate some of the other "expected"
frequencies to confirm the process. For a fiarly clear
explanation of the rationale behind this approach to
calculating expected frequencies in a contingency
table, see Daniel (1974, pp. 316-317).

With the expected frequencies before us, we
calculate chi-square as before, and find $\chi^2 = 13.69$.
To find the degrees of freedom, subtract one from the
number of rows and one from the number of columns and
multiply: $d.f. = (r - 1)(c - 1) = (4 \times 1) = 4$. A
chi-square table tells us that the probability of the
observed and expected frequencies being "really" the
same is less than one out of a hundred ($p < .01$). In
other words, the relative proportion in all cells of
children of Christian and non-Christian mothers is not
the same. It appears that the mother's religion
influences the child's view of God's discipline.

There is a problem, however. The small number
of people in the study ($n = 38$) will inflate the chi-
square. In a larger sample of the same type people,
the chi-square might not reach significance. For a

184

discussion of this problem, see Daniel (1974, p. 319).
Yates's correction can be applied to 2 x 2 contingency tables with small numbers of observations (see
Levin, 1973, pp. 194-196, or other statistics textbooks. Levin shows examples worked in detail),
although Daniel suggests that Yates's correction may
be too conservative.

The 2 x 2 contingency table is common enough
that it has a special chi-square computation formula
(easily derived from the regular chi-square formula).
Denote the cells as in Figure 9-5. Then,

$$\chi^2 = \frac{n(ad - bc)^2}{(a + c)(b + d)(a + b)(c + d)}$$

A	B	A+B
C	D	C+D
A+C	B+D	N

Figure 9-5.   The 2 X 2 contingency table for
chi-square analysis.

Fortney (1973, p.24) gives us a 2 x 2 example. Seminary students reported their mother's emotional outlook ("always or usually optimistic or happy" vs. "often or usually depressed or moody") and whether or not the mother was Christian or non-Christian. The observations are shown in Table 9-10.

Table 9-10

Mother's Emotional Outlook vs. Her Spiritual Status

(Demonstration of Chi-Square Calculation for 2x2 Table)

MOTHER'S SPIRITUAL STATUS	MOTHER'S EMOTIONAL OUTLOOK		
	HAPPY	MOODY	TOTAL
CHRISTIAN	18(16.8)	7(8.1)	25
NON-CHRISTIAN	9(10.1)	6(4.9)	15
TOTAL	27	13	40

$$x^2 = \frac{40(18\times6 - 7\times9)}{(27)(13)(25)(15)} = \frac{40(108 - 63)}{131,625} = \frac{1800}{131,625} = .0137$$

df = 1   not significant.

Note. Figures in parentheses are expected cell values.
Note. Data from William Boyd Fortney, (1973).

This analysis indicates that the mother's emotional state is not a function of whether or not she is a Christian. The variables are independent.

CHAPTER X

A FEW LOOSE ENDS: TOPICS IN DATA ANALYSIS

In this chapter we consider several miscellaneous problems.

Reporting Percentages

Probably the simplest form of data analysis is the calculation of percentages. We all learned about this powerful tool while we were in elementary school, but in spite of the fact that it is elementary, calculating and reporting percentages requires thought.

Zeisel (1968, chapter 1, 2, and 3) makes several points about the use of percentages, including these:

1. Percentages are designed to enhance the readibility of numerical findings. Sometimes the raw numbers are sufficiently readable.

2. Since the role of a percentage is to simplify a report, decimals should seldom be used in percentages.

3. If there are more than four columns, do not report both raw numbers and percentages in a table. Instead, report the base (total) from which the percentages were computed, so the reader can determine the original numbers if necessary.

4. When two variables are related in a table, "per cents should be computed in the direction of the causal factor, provided the sample is representative in that direction."

5. Reporting comparisons (increases or decreases) as percentages is frequently a dubious procedure because of the difficulty of choosing the appropriate base. The base may be any of the elements in the comparison, or it may be an element not found in the comparison at all.

187

Fortney (1973) provides examples for a discussion of the first four points. He raised an interesting question about the relationships among three variables: (a) the spiritual status of parents (saved/unsaved), (b) the relationship between the parents and the children, and (c) the relationship between the child and God. Such a study "makes sense" if the operationalizations are adequate, and at this point we will accept Fortney's operationalizations. The "children" that Fortney studied were all seminary students. They were asked to complete a questionnaire developed by Bruce Narramore and published in A Guide to Child Rearing; A Manual for Parents to Accompany "Help! I'm a Parent" (Zondervon, 1972). The Narramore questionnaire deals with feelings about how the respondent relates to father, mother and God. In addition, Fortney asked some informational questions, including whether or not the father and mother were Christian.

Fortney's data analysis consisted of inspecting relationships between responses for every possible pair of questionnaire items. One approach would be to calculate correlation coefficients (except in those instances when the data are nominal), but Fortney chose to present tables of percentages. This approach is somewhat tedious (most of the thesis consists of tables), but it does make a good case study in data analysis. In some cases tables force us to be aware of things we might miss if we were dealing only with correlation coefficients.

One of Fortney's tables (p. 39) reproduced here as Table 10-1 (see also Table 9-9, above). Following Zeisel's suggestions, we might revise Table 10-1 by eliminating the decimal points and eliminating the raw numbers (Table 10-2). Note that Table 10-2 adds a row for percentages of the total, allowing the reader to get a sense of where the discrepancy lies.

For this example, it would probably be as good to report the raw numbers without percentages. Furthermore, as we saw in Chapter 9, you can compute a chi-square from the raw numbers to determine the significance of relationship between the two variables.

Table 10-1

Mother's Spiritual Status Related To
Child's View of God's Discipline

	GOD'S DISCIPLINE				
MOTHER'S SPIRITUAL STATUS	INSUFFICIENT	FIRM, BUT SOMETIMES HARSH OR INCONSISTENT	FIRM, BUT LOVING	HARSH AT TIMES	ADEQUATE BASED ON RESPECT
CHRISTIAN	5 20.83%	1 4.16%	16 66.66%	0 0.00%	2 8.33%
NON-CHRISTIAN	2 14.28%	0 0.00%	3 21.42%	4 28.57%	5 35.71%

Note. Data from Communicating God's Character to Children by William Boyd Fortney, (1973) p. 39.

Table 10-2

Simplification of Table 10-1, Following Zeisel

	GOD'S DISCIPLINE					
MOTHER'S SPIRITUAL STATUS	INSUFFICIENT	FIRM, BUT SOMETIMES HARSH OR INCONSISTENT	FIRM, BUT LOVING	HARSH AT TIMES	ADEQUATE BASED ON RESPECT	TOTAL
CHRISTIAN	21%	4	67	0	8	100
NON-CHRISTIAN	14%	0	21	29	36	100
TOTAL	18%	3	50	11	18	100
NUMBER	7	1	19	4	7	38

Note. Based on communicating God's Character to Children by William Boyd Fortney, (1973), p.39.

189

Following Zeisel, we assume Fortney, by laying out his data as he did, anticipated that mother's spiritual state causes the child's view of God's discipline. Fortney's approach seems to be appropriate, but for the sake of illustration, compare the alternative way of calculating percentages (Table 10-3). In reporting percentages, give careful attention to what the base of your percentage calculation is.

Table 10-3

Alternative Method of Calculating Percentages
For Data in Table 10-1

MOTHER'S SPIRITUAL STATUS	GOD'S DISCIPLINE					
	INSUFFICIENT	FIRM, BUT SOMETIMES HARSH OR INCONSISTENT	FIRM, BUT LOVING	HARSH AT TIMES	ADEQUATE BASED ON RESPECT	TOTAL
CHRISTIAN	71%	100%	84%	0	29%	63%
NON-CHRISTIAN	29%	0	16%	100%	71%	37%
TOTAL	100%	100%	100%	100%	100%	100%
NUMBER	7	1	19	4	7	38

Black (1980, p. 89) provides an example for us of percentage comparisons. As part of his study, he asked 70 ministers (45 questionnaires returned) and 140 older church members (66 questionnaires returned) in four churches to respond on a Likert scale to the statement, "The church is using the professional knowledge of its older members as it should." He used a bar chart to report his findings (Figure 10-1). Some authors argue that bar charts do not add enough clarity to the figures to justify the space they require (American Psychological Association, 1974, p. 55). For your thesis, you must decide whether a figure, such as a bar chart, or a table of numbers would be better.

The comparison should be adequately made in the chart or table without attempting to assign a number to the differences. For example, which is the better interpretation?

(a) 25% more senior citizens than ministers agree with statement. (58% - 33% = 25%.)

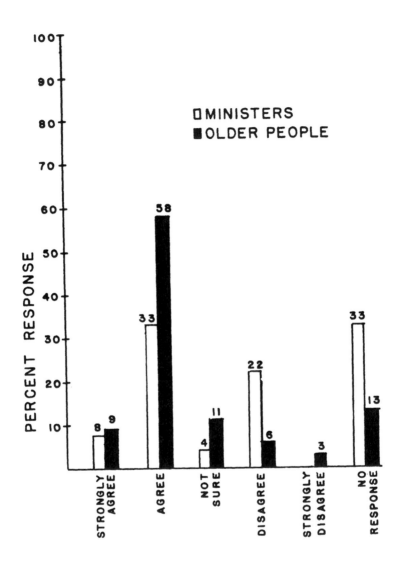

Figure 10-1.   Example of Bar Graph.   Comparison of
answers to the question: "The church is
using the professional knowledge of its
older members as it should."   Note.
From Older People in the Life of the
Church, by Wayne Black.

191

(b)   76% more senior citizens than ministers
      agree with the statement. (Here we assume
      the 33% of ministers who agree constitute
      the base. 76% of 33 = 25, and 25 + 33 =
      58.)

Neither of these approaches is "incorrect," and you
will not get clear agreement as to which is best.

Notes On Surveying Priorities

        Probably the most common form of survey in the
local church is the priority survey in which you
establish a list of potential activities and ask
people with an interest in the activities to rank them
from most important to least important. Simple as
such a survey is, there are considerations that will
increase its validity and usefulness.

Preparing the List

        You can write the list in the quiet of your
study, or you can assign the task to a committee. In
many, if not most, situations, this method is adequate,
but you also may miss some options that should be part
of the list.

        Another approach is to modify the "Delphi
technique." this technique was developed as a way of
studying the probable future of an institution, thus
the name. Many Delphi studies have been done, and
many articles commenting on the technique have been
written. These can be found by consulting the various
standard indexes, such as Psychological Abstracts, and
Dissertation Abstracts International.

        The Delphi technique is essentially a search for
consensus among experts. One way to modify the Delphi
technique to develop a priority questionnaire is as
follows:

        Select a group of several "experts," each
qualified to write a priority list. Do not call them
together as a committee, or even tell any of them who
the others are. Ask each to prepare a priority list.

Compile the lists, indicating beside each suggested
item how many experts suggested it. Send this compilation to each expert asking them to (a) indicate those
items which should definitely be on the survey (you
may ask for the top ten, or some such number), and
(b) suggest any new items that come to mind. These
responses may provide your survey form, or you may
want to go through another round.

This is a fairly complex process, but in some
cases definitely useful.

Helping People Complete the Survey

If the list is long, or involves fine distinctions, people may have a hard time putting them in
priority order. If you are conducting individual
interviews, it might help to have the items on cards,
and ask the people to stack the cards with the most
important item on top.

Another approach is to have them consider all
possible pairs of items. A five item survey form
would resemble Figure 10-2.

Figure 10-2.

Format for Paired Responses

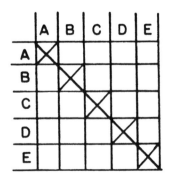

Ask people to place a "y" (for "yes)" in the box
if they consider the item in the column to be more
important than the item in the row. Note that one
side of the diagonal will be the "mirror image" of the
other. Then ask them to count the number of "y's" in
each row. The more "y's," the higher the priority.
For example, see Figure 10-3:

Figure 10-3

Sample Paired Responses

ARE THESE LESS IMPORTANT ?

ARE THESE MORE IMPORTANT ?	A	B	C	D	E	NUMB. OF "Y's"
A		Y		Y		2
B			Y	Y	Y	3
C	Y					1
D		Y				1
E	Y		Y	Y		3

According to the responses in Fig.10-3, B and E
are tied for first priority, C and D are tied for last
priority, and A is in the middle.

This technique does allow for ties, and we might
consider it to be a good feature. If the respondent
is really ambivalent about the priority ranking of
two or more items, is it valid to force that person
to make an artifical choice?

Note in Fig.10-4 that it is possible for a respondent to make no priority decisions:

194

Figure 10-4

Paired Responses with No Priority

	A	B	C	D	E	NUMB. OF "Y's"
A		Y		Y		2
B				Y	Y	2
C	Y	Y				2
D			Y		Y	2
E	Y		Y			2

How to Handle Ties

Consider the example in Fig. 10-3. On a scale of one through five, how should each item be numbered? The answer is:

$$
\begin{array}{ll}
B & 1.5 \\
E & 1.5 \\
A & 3 \\
C & 4.5 \\
D & 4.5
\end{array}
$$

If you have tied ranks, average the scores the tied responses represent, and assign the average score to each of them.

Reducing Many Responses to One

Once you have everyone's response, average all of the responses for each item. Arrange the resulting numbers in numerical order. Handle ties as indicated in the above section. Table 4 presents an example without ties, and Table 5 presents an example with ties:

Table 10-4

Priority Responses Without Ties
Between Respondents

ITEM	RESPONDENT				AVERAGE	RANK
	Sam	Agnes	George	Sue		
A	3	4	2.5	3	3.1	3
B	1.5	1	2.5	1	1.5	1
C	4.5	2	4	4.5	4.75	4
D	4.5	5	5	4.5	4.75	5
E	1.5	3	1	2	1.8	2

Table 10-5

Priority Responses With Ties
Between Respondents

ITEM	RESPONDENT				AVERAGE	RANK
	Glen	Bob	Jane	Joyce		
A	2.5	1.5	3.5	1	2.1	2.5
B	1	1.5	2	2	1.6	1
C	4	4.5	5	4	4.3	5
D	5	4.5	5	4	4.3	5
E	2.5	2	1	3	2.1	2.5

196

How Much Agreement is There on the Priority Ranking?

You can measure agreement among the people ranking the priorities by calculating the Kendall Coefficient of Concordance, also called "Kendall's W." The calculation is not difficult. The technique is explained fully in Nonparametric Statistics for the Behavioral Sciences by Sidney Siegel (New York: McGraw-Hill Book Company, 1956, pp. 229-238. This book is still in print!)

Siegel's discussion is readable with examples and a minimum of mathematical notation. Anyone willing to take the time to work through the examples should be able to master the calculations.

If we combine the eight respondents from Tables 4 and 5 into one list, we calculate W = .742 (corrected for ties). This indicates a high degree of agreement among them. For total agreement, W = 1. For the strongest possible disagreement, W = 0.

In the above reference, Siegel describes a significance test for W that gives you the probability of W being greater than would be achieved by chance. In a formal study, such as a D.Min. thesis, you should compute the significance level.

Other Techniques for Studying Phenomena

We have considered only those techniques for obtaining and analyzing information that seem useful for the most common D. Min. projects. If you have a special problem you want to investigate, visit a major university and talk to as many people as you can about it. Someone will know of a way to handle your problem.

One of the special problems we have barely mentioned is "forecasting," including "time series analysis" and the "Delphi technique." Chambers, Mullick and Smith (1974, chap. 3) provide a readable overview of qualitative and quantitative forecasting methods.

We mentioned the delphi technique in the above section on surveying priorities. This is probably the most useful forecasting method for D. Min. research. The idea behind it is that when you use a panel of experts who are unaware of one another, you get the benefit of their knowledge (and wisdom) without having their judgement influenced by personality dynamics. The consensus achieved after several rounds of surveying the panel is, in theory, the best possible consensus.

With time series analysis, you can study attendance trends, membership trends, or other trends for which you have historical data. There are several techniques of time series analysis, and they are all controversial because unexpected events can drastically change the future. The study can only tell you what might happen, not what will happen.

Time series analysis was developed as a business management technique (how many units of our product can we expect to sell next quarter), but it is now being used for non-business applications, such as program evaluation (Forehand, 1982). Schoenherr and Sorensen (1982) provide an example. They used time series analysis to study clergy trends in the Catholic church. For a simple example of time series analysis, see Chapter 2, Figure 2-2.

SCALES FROM THE RELIGIOUS BELIEF INVENTORY
                    from
R. R. Lee, Theological Belief as a Dimension of
    Personality, Ph.D. Dissertation, Northwestern
    University, 1965. (reproduced by permission.)

Note: Each scale consists of eight items. A person who
       received a high score for the scale will agree
       with four items and disagree with four items.
       When structured for test purposes, items from
       various scales should be "scrambled" in random
       order.

HUMANISM, "agree" items:

SA A U D SD -- The major function of religion is the
                 integration of personality.

SA A U D SD ◦-- Man has proved adequate as the central
                 concern of society.

SA A U D SD -- Man is not sinful, merely foolish.

SA A U D SD -- The way to build a better society is
                 to appeal to people's reason.

HUMANISM, "disagree" items:

SA A U D SD -- An open mind is an appealing but un-
                 realistic goal.

SA A U D SD -- Authority of the State rests on more
                 than just the consent of the people.

SA A U D SD -- All major religions teach different
                 basic beliefs.

SA A U D SD -- Man is quite incapable of setting and
                 achieving his own goals.

FUNDAMENTALISM, "agree" items:

SA A U D SD -- All these modern translations of
                 Scripture present a real threat to
                 the Gospel.

SA A U D SD -- We know that God forgives us our sins because Christ gave His life as substitute for us.

SA A U D SD -- After Jesus arose from the dead, He walked, talked, and ate with the disciples.

SA A U D SD -- When Joshua commanded the sun to stand still, it did so.

FUNDAMENTALISM, "disagree" items:

SA A U D SD -- At Cana, Jesue did not literally turn water into wine.

SA A U D SD -- Jesus Christ was born by natural procreation.

SA A U D SD -- The Bible is fallible.

SA A U D SD -- Adam and Eve are not historical persons.

PURITANISM, "agree" items:

SA A U D SD -- The world is full of demonic forces which seek to control our lives.

SA A U D SD -- Alcohol is a dangerous agent of misery and vice.

SA A U D SD -- Life in this world is a constant struggle against evil and wickedness.

SA A U D SD -- It is a sin to play any sport or do any work on the Sabbath.

PURITANISM, "Disagree" items:

SA A U D SD -- There is nothing intrinsically wrong in smoking.

SA A U D SD -- Cardplaying is a harmless pastime.

SA A U D SD -- Dancing is a normal, healthy, social activity.

SA A U D SD -- Providing a person stays within his financial means, gambling is harmless.

PIETISM, "Agree" items:

SA A U D SD -- Setting aside a portion of each day for family prayer and meditation is a part of Christian living.

SA A U D SD -- All preaching ought to include an
              urgent appeal for conversion.

SA A U D SD -- No one can be a Christian unless he
              has a personal relationship with
              Jesus Christ.

SA A U D SD -- A large proportion of the Church's
              mission and money ought to be directed
              towards the poor, the ill-educated and
              underprivileged, both at home and
              abroad.

PIETISM, "disagree" items:

SA A U D SD -- Small, regular, mid-seek meetings for
              prayer, study and discussion are an
              appendix to the major purpose of the
              church.

SA A U D SD -- Christianity is more a philosophy or
              a system of beliefs than a way of
              living.

SA A U D SD -- The experience of a new birth is un-
              necessary for membership in the Church.

SA A U D SD -- God's ministers are only those who
              are ordained by the church.

SCIENTISM, "Agree" items:

SA A U D SD -- Man's primary concern ought to be
              with the laws of nature.

SA A U D SD -- One day science will supersede
              religion.

SA A U D SD -- What we know can only come to us
              through the five senses.

SA A U D SD -- When compared with the vastness of
              space and the power of the atom, man
              fades into insignificance.

SCIENTISM, "disagree" items:

SA A U D SD -- There are other types of knowledge
              which outweigh scientific knowledge.

SA A U D SD -- Science is inadequate to ultimately
              overcome all the problems of society.

SA A U D SD   --   The trouble with science is that it
                   has structured the world in a cold,
                   impersonal way.

SA A U D SD   --   Science should have little concern
                   for such things as ultimate truth or
                   reality.

SCORING: For "agree" items, SA = 4, A = 3, U = 2,
           D = 1, and SD = 0. for "disagree" items,
           SA = 0, A = 1, U = 2, D = 3, and SD = 4.
           Thus, scale scores range from 0 to 32.

The following table gives means and standard
deviations for the scores of four groups on these
five scales.

	United Methodist laity, 1975 $\underline{n} = 147$	Garrett Seminary students, 1965 $\underline{n} = 302$	Northwestern U. undergrads, 1965 $\underline{n} = 111$	Atheists & agnostics, 1965 $\underline{n} = 26$
Humanism				
mean	15.68	12.55	18.14	19.38
std. dev.	3.81	4.42	4.16	4.53
Fundamentalism				
mean	18.78	14.15	15.15	6.15
std. dev.	5.39	5.54	7.01	3.75
Puritanism				
mean	16.32	12.62	10.59	8.93
std. dev.	5.35	3.84	4.62	4.28
Pietism				
mean	21.18	18.75	13.45	11.57
std. dev.	4.11	4.08	3.97	4.09
Scientism				
mean	11.50	8.37	12.87	16.60
std. dev.	3.56	3.27	4.35	3.71

Source of above is Lee (1965, p. 60) and Davies (1975, p. 54).

CONCEPT EVALUATION TEST
(AN EXAMPLE OF ORDINAL MEASUREMENT)
from

J. A. Privette, <u>A Study of Factors in the Understanding</u>
Ed.D. Dissertation, Southern Baptist Theological
Seminary, 1972. (reproduced by permission.)

<u>Instructions</u>: Below there are twelve questions, each
followed by six possible answers. Please read and
follow these directions for each of the questions:

1. Read the question.
2. Read <u>ALL</u> of the statements which follow the
   question.
3. Go back and place a <u>CHECK MARK</u> ( ) by the <u>ONE</u>
   statement which you feel is the <u>BEST</u> answer to
   the question.
4. Be sure to check <u>ONLY ONE STATEMENT</u> FOR EACH
   QUESTION.

1. WHO IS GOD?
   - __5__ God is the maker of heaven and earth.
   - __4__ God is the father of Jesus Christ.
   - __0__ God is someone who accepts you to come to
     live with him.
   - __1__ God is a man who lives in heaven, loves
     everybody, and made everything.
   - __2__ God is a spirit that cannot be seen.
   - __3__ God is our Saviour and Lord.

2. WHO IS JESUS?
   - __3__ Jesus is God's Son.
   - __4__ Jesus is God's only Son who died on the cross.
   - __0__ Jesus is a great man, a very important man
     who people believe in.
   - __5__ Jesus is our personal Saviour who died on
     the cross for our sins.
   - __2__ Jesus is a kind loving friend and a perfect
     human man.
   - __1__ Jesus is the one who could make the blind to
     see.

3. WHAT IS SIN?
   - __2__ Sin is when you do something that is not
     right.
   - __3__ Sin is when you are tempted by the devil to
     do wrong.
   - __1__ Sin is when you do not abey your parents.
   - __0__ Sin is being afraid of something.
   - __4__ Sin is something you do against God's will.

206

  5   Sin is rebelling against God.

4. WHAT IS GOD'S GRACE?
    1   God shed his grace on thee.
    0   God's grace is to say a prayer to God
        before you eat.
    2   God's grace is the kind things God does for
        us.
    4   God's grace is God's unfailing forgiveness
        and mercy.
    3   God's grace is God's love and understanding
        for us.
    5   God's grace is the free gift of God which
        is given to us because of God's love.

5. WHAT DOES IT MEAN TO BE SAVED?
    5   To be saved means to be born again.
    4   To be saved means to know Jesus and commit
        your life to him.
    2   To be saved means not to be lost.
    1   To be saved means you have been saved from
        hell.
    0   To be saved means to be baptized.
    3   To be saved means to trust God and let
        Jesus come into your life.

6. WHAT DOES IT MEAN TO BE LOST?
    1   To be lost means that you don't feel right.
    0   To be lost means that you feel that God is
        not with you.
    3   To be lost means that you are not going to
        heaven when you die.
    5   To be lost means not to trust or believe in
        Jesus as your Saviour.
    2   To be lost means not to be saved.
  NOTE: No response scored "4" was printed for this
        question.

7. WHAT DOES IT MEAN TO TRUST OR BELIEVE IN JESUS?
    2   This means that you must do what he wants
        you to do.
    4   This means to take him in your heart and
        believe.
    1   This means to love God, Jesus, and everybody,
        and hate the devel.
    3   To trust or believe in Jesus means to have
        faith in God.
    0   To trust or believe in Jesus means not to
        ever sin or do bad things.

<u>   5   </u> To trust or believe in Jesus menas to know
Jesus is the Son of God and believe that he
died on the cross for our sins.

8. WHAT IS FORGIVENESS?
<u>   3   </u> Forgiveness means to forget and to love.
<u>   4   </u> Forgiveness means that you ask God to
forgive you.
<u>   2   </u> Forgiveness means when someone does some-
thing to you, you forgive them and say,
"That's all right."
<u>   0   </u> Forgiveness means to take back what you said.
<u>   5   </u> Forgiveness means that when you ask Jesus
to forgive you of your sins, he will cleanse
you.
<u>   1   </u> Forgiveness means if you steal something
from somebody and you give it back, they
forgive you for it.

9. WHY DO PEOPLE CALL JESUS THE SAVIOUR OF THE WORLD?
<u>   4   </u> Jesus is called the Saviour because he
saves you.
<u>   0   </u> Jesus is called the Saviour because he heals
people.
<u>   1   </u> Jesus is called the Saviour because he
performs miracles.
<u>   5   </u> Jesus is called the Saviour because he gave
his life for us.
<u>   2   </u> Jesus is called the Saviour because he
loves you.
<u>   3   </u> Jesus is called the Saviour because he came
to earth to save the world from sin.

10. WHAT DOES IT MEAN TO ACCEPT CHRIST?
<u>   3   </u> To accept Christ means just ask the Lord to
come into your heart.
<u>   5   </u> To accept Christ means to take him as your
personal Saviour.
<u>   0   </u> To accept Christ means to get baptized.
<u>   2   </u> To accept Christ means that Christ is a
friend that you like.
<u>   1   </u> To accept Christ means to believe that there
is a God.
<u>   4   </u> To accept Christ means to say that you want
him to have your life.

11. HOW DOES A PERSON KNOW WHEN HE SINS?
<u>   4   </u> Down in your heart God is telling you when
you sin.

_1_ When a person sins he just knows something is wrong.

_3_ When we sin, it hurts our conscience.

_5_ A person knows when he sins because he gets hurt or he gets in trouble.

_0_ You know when you have sinned because you recognize that what you have done is wrong.

_2_ When a person sins, Christ convicts him.

12. WHAT DOES IT MEAN TO COMMIT YOUR LIFE TO CHRIST?

_5_ To commit your life to Christ means to give all to Christ.

_2_ To commit your life to christ means to have Christ call you to turn your life over to him.

_1_ To commit your life to Christ means to do kind things.

_4_ To commit your life to Christ means to let him take your life and let him do what God thinks is best for you.

_3_ To commit your life to christ means to say you believe and love Christ in your heart.

_0_ You commit your life to Christ when you have risen from the grave.

"Concept Evaluation Test" reproduced with permission of Jerry A. Privette from his dissertation, A Study of Factors in the Understanding of Salvation-Related Concepts in Preadolescent Children from Three Southern Baptist Churches. Louisville: Southern Baptist Theologocial Seminary, 1972, pp. 112-115.

BIBLIOGRAPHY

Allport, Gordon W. The individual and his religion.
New York: Macmillan, 1954.

American Psychological Association. Publication manual
of the American Psychological Association (2nd
ed.). Washington, D.C.: Author, 1974.

Amidon, Edmund J. & Hough, John B. (Eds.). Interaction
analysis: Theory, research, and application.
Reading, Bass.: Addison-Wesley, 1967.

Armbrister, Trevor. The case of the two-bit dollar.
Reader's Digest, January 1980, pp. 128-130.

Bailis, Lawrence R., & Kennedy, William R. Effects of
a death education program upon secondary school
students. The Journal of Educational Research,
1977, 71(2), 63-66.

Barron, Frank, & Harrington, David M. Creativity,
intellegence and personality. In M. R. Rosenzweig & L. W. Porter (Eds.), Annual Review of
Psychology (Vol. 32)., Palo Alto, CA: Annual
Reviews, Inc., 1981.

Bass, William L. A project in leadership development
for a local church's inistry of evangelism
through small group interaction. Unpublished
doctoral dissertation (D. Min.), Christian
Theological seminary, 1977.

Berelson, Bernard. Content analysis in communication
research. New York: The Free Press of Glencoe,
1952.

Berkouwer, G. C. [Studies in dogmatics; Faith and
justification] (Lewis B. Smedes, trans.).
Grand rapids, MI: Wm. B. Eerdmans, 1954.

Birkos, Alexamder S., & Tambs, Lewis A. Historio-
graphy, method, history teaching; A bibliography
of books and articles in English, 1965-1973.
Hamden, Conn.: Linnet Books, 1975.

Black, Wayne. Older people in the life of the church.
Unpublished doctoral dissertation (D. Min.),
Christian Theological Seminary, 1980.

211

Bloesch, Donald G. Essentials of evangelical theology;
Volume two: Life, ministry, and hope. San
Francisco: Harper & Row, 1979.

Bonjean, C., McLemore, D., & Hill, R. Sociological
measurement. San Francisco: Chandler, 1967.

Budd, Richard W., Thorp, Robert K., & Donohew, Lewis.
Content analysis of communications. New York:
Macmillan, 1967.

Buros, Oscar Krisen.(Ed.). The eighth mental measurements yearbook (2 vols.)., Highland Park, N.J.:
Gryphon Press, 1978.

Cain, Glen G., & Hollister, Robinson G. The methodology of evaluating social action programs. In
Peter H. Rossi & Walter Williams (Eds.),
Evaluating social programs: Theory, practice,
politics. New York: Seminar Press, 1972.

Campbell, Donald T., & Stanley, Julian N. Experimen-
tal and quasi-experimental designs for research.
Chicago: Rand McNally, 1963. Also in Gage,
N. L. (Ed.). Handbook of research on teaching.
Chicago: Rand McNally, 1963.

Campbell, Stephen K. Flaws and fallacies in statistical thinking. Englewood Cliffs, N.J.:
Prentice-Hall, 1974.

Campbell, Thomas C., & Fukuyama, Yoshio. The fragmented layman: An empirical study of lay
attitudes. Philadelphia: Pilgrim Press, 1970.

Carr, John Crosbie. The MMPI, ministerial personality,
and the practice of ministry (Doctoral dissertation, Northwestern University, 1980). Dissertation Abstracts International, (University Microfilms No. 80-26,776)

Cattell, Raymond B. The scientific use of factor
analysis in behavioral and life sciences. New
York: Plenum, 1978.

Chambers, John C., Mullick, Satinder K., & Smith,
Donald D. An executive's guide to forecasting.
New York: John Wiley, 1974.

212

Clingan, Donald F. Let your light shine: A research study measuring the impact of one-day older adult retreats and a twelve-week small group experience on older persons. Unpublished doctoral dissertation (D. Min.), Christian Theological Seminary, 1978.

Cofield, Dama C. A study of numinous experience. Unpublished M.A. thesis, Butler University, Indianapolis, IN, 1965.

Conte, Hope R., Weiner, Marcella B., & Plutchik, Robert. Measuring death anxiety: Conceptual, psychometric and factor-analytic aspects. Journal of Personality and Social Psychology, 1982, 43, 775-785.

Conway, Sister Gilchrist. Crises in contemporary Catholic ecclesiology. Unpublished doctoral dissertation (D. Min.), Christian Theological SEminary, 1975.

Corbett, Warren G. Developing and testing a plan for evaluating the experience of church education and Christian instruction in the life of a congregation, Unpublished doctoral dissertation (D. Min.), Christian Theological Seminary, 1979.

Coville, Walter J., et al. Assessment of Candidates for the Religious Life: Basic Psychological Issues and Procedures. Washington, D.C.: Center for Applied Research in the Apostolate, 1968.

Crumbaugh, J. C. The seeking of noetic goals test (SONG): A complementary scale to the purpose-in-life test (PIL). Journal of Clinical Psychology, 1977, 33, 900-907.

Daniel,Wayne W. Biostatistics: A foundation for analysis in the health sciences. New York: John Wiley, 1974.

Darwin,Charles Williams, Jr. A group approach to integrating the Bible and marriage growth in the local church. Unpublished doctor dissertation (D. Min.), Christian Theological Seminary, 1976.

213

Davies, Richard. Creative ambiguity. <u>Religious</u>
<u>Education</u>, 1982, <u>77</u>, 642-656.

Davies, Richard. <u>Measurement in religious education</u>.
Paper presented at the International Convention
of the Religious Education Association, Nov.
20-22, 1977, St. Louis, MO. (ERIC Document
Reproduction Service No. ED 170 300)

Dillman, Don A. <u>Mail and telephone surveys: The</u>
<u>total design method</u>. New York: John Wiley, 1978.

Douglas-Smith, Basil. An empirical study of religious
mysticism. <u>British Journal of Psychiatry</u>,
1971, <u>118</u>, 549-554.

Dykstra, Craig R. <u>Vision and character: A Christian</u>
<u>educator's alternative to Kohlberg</u>. New York:
Paulist Press, 1981.

Embree, Robert A. The Religious Association Scale:
A preliminary validation study. <u>Journal for the</u>
<u>Scientific Study of Religion</u>, 1973, <u>12</u>, 223-226.

Enyart, David A. <u>Vocation as ministry</u>. Unpublished
doctoral dissertation (D. Min.), Christian
Theological Seminary, 1978.

Espy, R. H. Edwin. <u>The religion of college teachers</u>.
New York, Association Press, 1951.

Fairchild, Roy W., & Wynn, John C. <u>Families in the</u>
<u>church: A Protestant survey</u>. New York:
Association Press, 1961.

Feagin, J. "Prejudice and religious types: A focused
study of southern fundamentalists. <u>Journal for</u>
<u>the Scientific Study of Religion</u>, 1964, <u>4</u>, 3-13.
Flannery Clyde D. <u>A Bible skills workshop</u>. Unpublished doctoral dissertation (D. Min.), Christian
Theological Seminary, 1976.

Forehand, Garlie A. (Ed.). <u>Application sof time series</u>
<u>analysis to evaluation</u>. San Francisco: Jossey-
Bass, 1982.

Fortney, William Boyd. <u>Communicating God's character</u>
<u>to children</u>. Unpublished Master's thesis,
Dallas Tehological Seminary, 1973.

Fowler, James W. Stages of faith: The psychology of human development and the quest for meaning. San Francisco: Harper & Row, 1981.

Gelpi, Donald L. Experiencing God: A theology of human experience. New York: Paulist Press, 1978.

Glass, Gene V., & Stnaley, Julian C. Statistical methods in education and psychology. Englewood Cliffs, N.J.: Prentice-Hall, 1970.

Glass, J. Conrad, Jr. Ministerial job satisfaction scale. Review of Religious Research, 1976, 17, 153-157.

Glock, Charles Y., & Stark, Rodney. Christian beliefs and anti-semitism. New York: Harper & Row, 1966.

Glock, Charles Y., & Stark, Rodney. Religion and society in tension. Chicago: Rand McNally, 1965.

Gould, Stephen J. The mismeasure of man. New York: W. W. Norton, 1981.

Greeley, Andrew M., McCready, William C., & McCourt, Kathleen. Catholic schools in a declining church. Kansas City: Sheed & Ward, 1976.

Haburn, William B. A factor analysis of professional competencies and local church clergy (Doctoral dissertation, Oregon State University, 1976). Dissertation Abstracts International, 1976, (University Microfilms No. 76-23,518)

Hart, Geraldine, Ames, Kenneth A., & Sawyer, Robert N. Philosophical positions of nuns and former nuns: A discriminant analysis. Psychological Reports, 1974, 35, 675-678.

Hartshorne, Hugh. Character in human relations. New York: Scribner's, 1932.

Havelock, Ronald G. et al. Planning for innovation through dissemination and utilization of know-ledge. Ann Arbor, MI: Center for Research on Utilization of Scientific Knowledge, Institute for Social Research, University of Michigan,

215

n.d. (second printing, 1971).

Heeg, Harmen. Word and situation in Reformed preaching. Unpublished doctoral dissertation (D.
Min.), Christian Theological Seminary, 1978.

Hoge, Dean R., Dyble, John E., & Polk, David T.
Organizational and situational influences on
vocational commitment of Protestant minister.
Review of Religious Research, 1981, 23, 133-149.

Hood, Ralph W., Jr. The construction and preliminary
validation of a measure of reported mystical
experience. Journal for the Scientific Study of
Religion, 1975, 14, 29-41.

Huff, Darrell. How to lie with statistics. New York:
W. W. Norton, 1954.

Hunt, Richard A., & King, Morton B. The intrinsic-
extrinsic concept: A review and evaluation.
Journal for the Scientific Study of Religion,
1971, 10, 339-356.

Hunter, James Davison. Operationalizing evangelicalism: A review, critique and proposal.
Sociological Analysis, 1981, 42, 363-372.

Isaac, Stephen, & Michael, William B. Handbookin
research and evaluation San Diego, CA: Robert
R. Knapp, Publisher, 1971.

Jackson, Douglas N., & Paunonen, Sampo V. Personality
sturcture and assessment. In M. R. Rosenzweig
& L. W. Porter (Eds.), Annual Review of Psychol-
gy (Vol. 31). Palo Alto, CA: Annual Reviews,
Inc., 1980.

Jackson, Edgar N. A psychology for preaching. Great
Neck, NY: Channel Press, 1961.

Jensen, Arthur R. Bias in mental testing. New York:
Free Press, 1980.

Johns-Heine, Patrick, & Gerth, Hans H. Values in mass
periodical fiction, 1921-1940. Public Opinion
Quarterly, 1949, 13, 105-113.

Joy, Donald M. (Ed.) Moral development foundations: Judeo-Christian alternatives to Piaget-Kohlberg. Nashville: Abingdon, 1983.

Katona, George. The role of the frame of reference in war and post-war economy. American Journal of Sociology, 1944, 49, 340-347.

Kerlinger, Fred N. Foundations of behavioral reserach (2nd ed.). New York: Holt, Rinehart & Winston, 1973.

King, Morton B., & Hunt, Richard A. Measuring the religious variable: National replication. Journal for the Scientific Study of Religion, 1975, 14, 13-22.

Kirk, Roger E. Experimental design: Procedures for the behavioral sciences (2nd ed.). Belmont, CA: Brooks/Cole, 1982.

Kohlberg, Lawrence. Essays on moral development (Vol. 1), The philosophy of moral development: Moral stages and the idea of justice. San Francisco: Harper & Row, 1981.

Kurtines, William, & Pimm, June B. The moral development scale: A Piagetian measure of moral judgement. Educational and Psychological Measurement, 1983, 43, 89-105.

Lee, Ronald R. Theological belief as a dimension of personality (Doctoral dissertation, Northwestern University, 1965). Dissertation Abstracts International, 1965, (University Microfilms No. 65-12, 120)

Lemish, Peter S., & Lemish Dafna. A guide to the literature of qualitative research. Journal of Broadcasting, 1982, 26, 839-846.

Leo, J. From mollusks to moppets. Time, September 29, 1980, p. 55.

Levin, Jack. Elementary statitstics in social research. New York: Harper & Row, 1973.

Ligon, Ernest Mayfield. Their future is now: The growth and development of Christian personality. New York: Macmillan, 1939.

217

Macquarrie, John. Principles of Christian theology. New York: Scribners, 1966.

Mager, Robert F. Preparing instructional objectives. Belmont, CA: Fearon Pub., 1962.

McBrien, Richard P. Catholicism (Vol. II). Minneapolis: Winston Press, 1980.

McGavran, Donald A. Understanding church growth. Grand Rapids, MI: William B. Eerdmans Pub. Co., 1970.

Menges, Robert J. & Dittes, James E. Psychological Studies of Clergymen: Abstracts of Research. New York: Thomas Nelson & Sons, 1965.

Miller, Delbert C. Handbook of research design and social measurement (2nd ed.). New York: David McKay Co., 1970.

Mosteller, Frederick. Errors: Nonsampling errors. In David L. Sills (Ed.), International encyclopedia of the social sciences (Vol. 5). n.p.: Macmillan and Free Press, 1968.

Nelsen, Hart M., & Potvin, Raymond H. Gender and regional differences in the religiosity of Protestant adolescents. Review of Religious Research, 1981, 22, 268-285.

Osgood, Charles E., May, William H. & Miron, Murray S. Cross-cultural universals of affective meaning. Urbana: University of Illinois Press, 1975.

Peatling, John H. (Ed.). Annual review of research: Religious education (2 vols.). Schenectady, NY: Character Research Press, 1980-1981.

Peck, Jane C. A model for ministry. The Christian Century, 1983, 100, 94-97.

Phillips, Walter M. Purpose in life, depression and locus of control. Journal of Clinical Psychology, 1980, 36, 661-667.

Piaget, Jean. The moral judgement of the child. Glencoe, IL: Free Press, 1932.

Pulaski, Mary Ann Spencer. Understanding Piaget. New York: Harper & Row, 1971.

Reker, Gary T. & Peacock, Edward J. The life attitude profile (LAP): A multidimensional instrument for assessing attitudes toward life. Canadian Journal of Behavioral Science, 1981, 13, 264-273.

Rest, James R. Development in judging moral issues. Minneapolis: University of Minnesota Press, 1979.

Robinson, John P., & Shaver, Philip R. Measures of social psychological attitudes (Rev. ed.). Ann Arbor, Michigan: Survey Research Center, Institute for Social Research, 1973.

Rogers, Everett M. Diffusion of innovations. New York: Free Press, 1962.

Ross, Murray G. Religious beliefs of youth. New York: Association Press, 1950.

Rummel, R. J. Applied factor analysis. Evanston, Ill: Northwestern University Press, 1970.

St. John, Margaret Seymour. Being saved: Accounts of religious experience in an Appalachian valley (Doctoral dissertation, University of Michigan, 1982). Dissertation Abstracts International, 1982, 43, 514-B. (University Microfilms No. DA8215092.)

Sarason, Irwin G., & Smith, Ronald E. Personality. In P. H. Mussen & M. R. Rosenzweig (Eds.), Annual Review of Psychology (Vol. 22). Palo Alto, CA: Annual Reviews, Inc., 1971.

Schmuck, Richard A., et al. Handbook of organization development in schools. n.p.: National Press Books (ISBN 0-87484-208-5), 1972.

Schoenherr, Richard A., & Sorensen, Annemette. Social change in religious organizations: Consequences of clergy decline in the U.S. Catholic church. Sociological Analysis, 1982, 43, 23-52.

Schroeder, W. Widick. Measuring the muse: Reflections on the use of survey methods in the study of religious phenomena. Review of Religious

Research, 1977, 18, 148-162

Schuller, David S., Strommen, Merton P, & Brekke, Milo
(Eds.). Ministry in America: A Report and
analysis, based on an in-depth survey of 47
denominations in the United States and Canada,
with interpretations by 18 experts. San
Francisco: Harper & Row, 1980.

Segundo, Juan L. [Grace and the human condition]
(John Drury, trans.). Maryknoll, NY: Orbis
Books, 1973.

Selman, Robert L., & Lieberman, Marcus. Moral education in the primary grades: An evaluation of
a developmental curriculum. Journal of Educational Psychology, 1975, 67, 712-716.

Sexton, M. J. Who is the school: A Photographic
profile of the organizational climate of an
inner-city school. Dissertation Abstracts,
1972, 33, 1387-A.

Sexton, M. J. Who is the school? The Phi Delta Kappan,
1973a, 54, 397-403.

Sexton, M. J. Who is the school? Philadelphia, PA.:
Westminister Press, 1973b.

Shaw, M. & Wright, J. Scales for the measurement of
attitudes. New York: McGraw-Hill, 1967.

Sheldon, Henry C. System of Christian doctrine (rev.
ed.). New York: Methodist Book Concern, 1903.

Siegel, Sidney. Nonparametric statistics for the
behavioral sciences. New York: McGraw-Hill,
1956.

Simon, Julian L. Basic research methods in social
science: The art of empirical investigation.
New York: Random House, 1969.

Smith, John K. Quantitative versus qualitative
research: An attempt to clarify the issue.
Educational Researcher, March 1983, pp. 6-13.

Smith Raymond G. Development of a semantic differential for use with speech related concepts.
Speech Monographs, 1959, 26, 263-272.

Smith, Raymond G. The message measurement inventory:
A profile for communication analysis.
Bloomington: Indiana University Press, 1978.

Snider, J. G., & Osgood, C. E. Semantic differential
technique: a sourcebook. Chicago: Aldine
Publishing Co., 1969.

Snider, Theodore M. An approach to an early career
support system for ministry. Unpublished
doctoral dissertation (D. Min.), Christian
Theological Seminary, 1976.

Stark, Rodney, & Glock, Charles Y. American piety:
The nature of religious commitment. Berkeley:
University of California Press, 1968.

Stark, Rodney, et al. Wayward shepherds: Prejudice
and the Protestant clergy. New York: Harper &
Row, 1971.

Strommen, Merton P. (Ed.). Research on religious
development: A comprehensive handbook. New
York: Hawthorn Books, 1971.

Strommen, Merton P., et al. A study of generations.
Minneapolis: Augsburg, 1972.

Strong, Augustus H. Systematic theology: A compendium
and commonplace-book designed for the use of
theological student: Volume II, the doctrine
of man. Philadelphia: American Baptist
Publication Society, 1907.

Sudman, Seymour & Bradburn, Norman M. Asking questions:
A practical guide to questionnaire design. San
Francisco: Jossey-Bass, 1982.

Thielicke, Helmut. [The trouble with the church: A
call for renewal] (John W. Doberstein, Ed. and
trans.). New York: Harper & Row, 1965.

Tillich, Paul. Systematic theology; Volume three:
Life and the spirit, history and the kingdom of
God. Chicago: University of Chicago Press,
1963.

Watson, Goodwin. Research in religious education. In
Philip H. Lotz (Ed.), Studies in religious education. Nashville, TN: Cokesbury, 1931.

Weiss, Carol H. Evaluation research: Methods for assessing program effectiveness. Englewood Cliffs, NJ: Prentice-Hall, 1972.

Whelan, Winifred, & Adler, Virginia. Survey concerning the relationship between DRE's and priests: Final report from the research and development committee submitted to the Chicago Association of Religious Educators (CARE), December 16, 1982.

Williams, Lloyd C. Clergy effectiveness training: A training program for increasing the counseling skills of clergymen. Unpublished doctoral dissertation (D. Min.), Christian Theological Seminary [1971?]

Willis, Joyce B., Feldman, Nina S. & Ruble, Diane N. Children's generosity as influenced by deservedness of reward and type of recipient. Journal of Educational Psychology, 1977, 69, 33-35.

Wilmoth, Gregory H., & McFarland, Sam G. A comparison of four measures of moral reasoning. Journal of Personality Assessment, 1977, 41, 396-401.

Zeisel, Hans. Say it with figures (5th ed.). New York: Harper & Row, 1968.